THE CELTS IN MYTH AND LEGEND

MYTHS OF THE WORLD

THE CELTS IN MYTH AND LEGEND

TIMOTHY R. ROBERTS

MetroBooks

MetroBooks

AN IMPRINT OF FRIEDMAN/FAIRFAX PUBLISHERS
©1995 by Michael Friedman Publishing Group, Inc.

Library of Congress Cataloging-in-Publication Data

Roberts, Timothy Roland, date
    The Celts in myth and legend / Timothy R. Roberts.
        p. cm. — (Myths of the world)
    Includes bibliographical references and index.
    ISBN 1-56799-092-4
    1. Celts. 2. Mythology, Celtic. I. Title. II. Series.
D70.R65 1995
299'. 16—dc20   94-13494
                                                CIP

Editor: Benjamin Boyington
Art Director: Jeff Batzli
Designer: Susan E. Livingston
Photography Editor: Susan Mettler

Color separations by HBM Print Pte. Ltd.
Printed in China by Leefung-Asco Printers Ltd.

For bulk purchases and special sales, please contact:
Friedman/Fairfax Publishers
Attention: Sales Department
15 West 26th Street
New York, NY 10010
212/685-6610 FAX 212/685-1307

PHOTOGRAPHY CREDITS

Art Resource: 11
Rita Bailey/Leo de Wys Inc.: 106
Adrian Baker/Leo de Wys Inc.: 108
Bridgeman/Art Resource, New York: 22
Britain on View: 69
Fridmar Damm/Leo de Wys Inc.: 23
Werner Forman Archive/Art Resource, New York: 29
Historical Pictures/Stock Montage: 104
Erich Lessing/Art Resource, New York: 2, 10, 13, 14, 15, 17, 19, 20, 21, 26, 30, 31, 44, 46, 48, 51, 53, 54, 56, 59, 64, 65, 68, 94
George Munday/Leo de Wyse Inc.: 40
Edmund Nagele/FPG International: 66, 87
New York Public Library: 18
David Noble/FPG International: 74, 80
North Wind Picture Archive: 8, 12, 16, 24, 25, 27, 28 bottom, 32, 35, 37, 38–39, 52, 55, 72, 76, 78, 85, 93, 97, 99, 102, 107
Nicolas Sapieha/Art Resource, New York: 6
Siena Artworks Ltd., ©Michael Friedman Publishing Group: 28 top, 36, 41, 43, 45, 47, 50, 57, 58, 61, 62, 63, 70, 77, 81, 82, 88, 89, 91, 95, 96, 101, 103
Steve Vidler/Leo de Wys Inc.: 71, 90, 98, 109

DEDICATION

For Iris and Morgan

CONTENTS

THE CELTS
ON THE CONTINENT

WHO WERE THE CELTS?

Even two millennia after their defeat by the Romans, at a time when their homeland has been reduced to Ireland and the western fringes of Great Britain, we encounter the Celtic (most authoritatively pronounced "keltic") world every day. If you are an aficionado of horror movies you have watched the unstoppable Michael Myers—who, it is revealed in *Halloween II*, is possessed by an ancient Celtic demon—hew his way through those gory

A Celtic warrior and a Roman soldier do battle in front of a conical Celtic hut. This stone relief is part of a column dedicated to the Emperor Antoninus Pius (A.D. 138–161), who led Roman campaigns against the Celts in Britain and Germany.

and brutal carnivals of blood, the *Halloween* movies. Even the holiday of Halloween traces its origins back to the yearly ancient Celtic celebration of Samhain, a time when the Celts believed the worlds of the dead and of the living became one.

Somewhat less dramatically, every time you use a handsaw or file, wash with soap, or eat bread made from flour that was ground in a rotary mill, you are using the inventions and technology of the Celts. The pioneers of North America rolled westward on iron-rimmed wagon wheels and harvested their wheat with a rotary reaper—again, both inventions of the Celts. Later, the standard track gauge of North American railroads was set at four feet eight and one-half inches—the structurally sound distance between the wheels of a Celtic chariot.

On a literary level, the legend of King Arthur, from Malory to the movies *Camelot* and *Monty Python and the Holy Grail*, is taken from an ancient Celtic source and still has the power to fascinate us. On the lighter side,

Albert Uderzo and Rene Goscinny's comic book series *Asterix* entertains millions with the adventures of the Celtic hero Asterix and his bumbling friend Obelix as they confound the Roman Army. A testament to its popularity is the fact that the comic is published in twenty-two languages, including Icelandic, Afrikaans, and Welsh. For the truly erudite or aggressively archaic, the comic book is even published in Latin.

On a more visual level, one of the most important contributions of the Celts has been their art; in a purely aesthetic sense, Celtic art stands out stylistically among the arts of ancient cultures. Unlike their Roman contemporaries, the Celts felt no need to record the practical or the real in their art. Roman art was the ultimate in realism; a man or woman was sculpted with loving attention to his or her flaws—scowls, pimples, and even moles were faithfully recorded. A painting of a tree or an animal (to judge from the few that have survived) was a faithful and exact copy of the real thing. Not so with Celtic art. The Celtic artist

This mythological animal, perhaps a representation of an elephant, adorns the lid of a bronze flask found at Durnberg, Austria. It was common practice for Celtic nobles to decorate the lids and handles of their drinking vessels with whimsical animal designs.

delighted in the abstract and the fantastic. Renderings of foxes, ducks, horses, and people were fanciful and fun, stylized and full of motion. On the Basse-Yutz flagons from circa 300 B.C., for example, the handles are abstractions of foxes chasing a duck up toward the spout. A vase from Nord Bavay, France, bearing a lifelike relief of a bearded man staring straight ahead seems to be an exercise in realism until one notices two more heads sprouting from his ears. And the Gundestrup Cauldron, a silver-plated bowl that was dredged out of a peat bog in Denmark, is covered with whimsical people and creatures cavorting on its inside and outside surfaces. One figure holds two deer by their hind legs, while on another part of the bowl a woman in what looks like a miniskirt dances with a dog. Elsewhere on the cauldron's surface a naked figure rides a fish, and a man wearing antlers holds a snake with a duck's head. We can only guess at what fascinating mythological stories lie behind these images.

The most well-known sources of Celtic art are the famous illuminated manuscripts of the European Dark Ages, which, while they reflect a Christian background, nevertheless continue the traditions of whimsical, and even comical, Celtic art within a technical framework that is truly amazing. For instance, *The Book of Kells* and the *Lindisfarne Gospels*, which date from the eighth century, contain hundreds of drawings and designs that illustrate the stories of the Christian Gospels. Often, the initial letter of a passage is formed of a mythical animal with an elongated body that runs down the entire page and legs and claws that range out and away from the animal's body and evolve into separate and equally fanciful designs. If the artwork were not so painstakingly rendered and laboriously colored, these initial letters could be mistaken for artists' doodles. Upon reflection, an artistic kinship between these medieval illustra-

tors and modern abstract painters becomes apparent—neither strives for an exact reproduction of a subject but for an expression of vitality and an outpouring of emotion.

The Romans and early Christian writers have left us a vivid account of the people who created this lively and unusual art. The Romans—who spent the first three hundred years of their recorded history fighting the Celts, until Julius Caesar beat them decisively at Alesia, Gaul, in 52 B.C.—painted a dark and terrifying picture of them. To the Romans, who seldom topped five and a half feet (1.6m), the Celts, who were generally at least

A page from *The Book of Kells* (c. A.D. 800), now housed in Trinity College, Dublin, Ireland, depicting Celtic art adapted to represent part of the Gospels (Luke 3:23–26). The Latin *Qui* ("who") on the left side of the page is repeated over and over again as part of the elongated body of a fierce-looking Celt whose body evolves into the heads and limbs of fantastic animals as it descends the page.

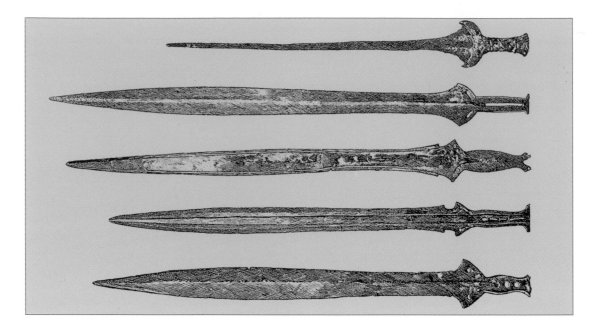

six feet (1.8m) tall, were almost giants. They painted and tattooed their bodies with strange designs, used lime to stiffen their long hair into spikes, and wore long, drooping mustaches that caught pieces of food when they ate. They fought sometimes in brightly colored, checkered tunics and pants, sometimes completely naked, wearing only the bizarre designs they had painted on their bodies—a practice the puritanical Romans found especially disturbing.

Despite the alarming portrait they painted of the Celts, the Romans nevertheless held a certain grudging admiration for these "primitives," for the Celts were great warriors, a trait the Romans respected above almost any other. In battle, the Celts fought with frenzied abandon, frothing at the mouth and swinging huge double-edged swords. Indeed, it was this frenzy that often defeated the Celts, for once their leaders launched them into battle, there was no way to maneuver them or control their actions. The more disciplined Romans, with their carefully trained armies, beat their more enthusiastic opponents time and time again. At Alesia, Caesar was able to defeat vastly larger numbers of Celts even though his Roman troops had to fight on two fronts at once. Also, Celtic courage was legendary. The Greek historian Posidonius (135–51 B.C.) once told the story of Alexander the Great asking a delegation of Celts what they most feared. They replied, "Only that the sky might crack open and fall on our heads."

When the Celts were not fighting Romans or Greeks, they fought one another in a bewildering number of wars and raids that were conducted as much for personal glory as for territorial expansion and financial gain. Even times of peace were not truly peaceful, for social occasions often degenerated into brawls. Each warrior at a banquet was seated by precedent, according to his skill and renown as a warrior, and anyone could challenge that precedent either by bragging about his military prowess until everyone agreed to a new seating arrangement or, as happened more often, by pulling out his sword and fighting for a new seat. Once the seating was settled, the next cause for concern was who would receive the "hero's portion." The favorite food of the Celts was roast boar, and the rear haunches of that animal were, by custom, reserved for the bravest warriors. Bravery was determined, of course, not by an official scorekeeper but by an ongoing series of challenges. A good portion of Celtic mythology is, in fact, built around these "beer hall brawls."

In the myth entitled Mac Da Tho's Boar, three heroes, along with their retainers, attend a great feast given by King Mac Da Tho of Leinster. The centerpieces of this feast are a collection of seven huge cauldrons filled with meat, and a boar of such prodigious size that forty oxen were required to haul the carcass to the feast hall. The common warriors are given the meat from the cauldrons, and the heroes are awarded the boar. The warrior Cet of the kingdom of Connacht, assuming that he is entitled to the boar because he is the greatest warrior present, steps forward with drawn knife to slice off a choice portion. He is immediately challenged by Loeguire of Ulster. Cet reminds Loeguire of their last meeting in a border skirmish, during which Loeguire lost his chariot, horses, and driver. When Cet resumes his slicing he is once more interrupted, but this time it is Oengus who challenges Cet's right to the hero's portion. Cet wins this exchange by reminding Oengus that he once

cut off Oengus' father's hand in battle; Oengus sits back down. Before Cet can resume cutting, another warrior, Eogan the One-eyed, challenges Cet. But when Cet reminds Eogan that he is one-eyed because of Cet's skill with the spear, Eogan thinks better of his challenge and sits down. In quick succession, three more heroes challenge Cet; Cet reminds each that he bears an infirmity caused by battle with Cet—one has lost a foot, another has lost his testicles, and still another has damaged vocal cords and so must speak in a high, squeaky voice unbecoming to a true hero.

By now the rest of the feasters are enjoying the verbal give-and-take of Cet and his challengers. Cet himself is also enjoying the exchanges, and after verbally defeating each challenger he yells, "Another challenger or I begin the cutting!" Finally, when everyone has had his chance, Cet puts his knife to the flesh only to be interrupted once again—this time by a new arrival to the feast, Connall

This small bronze figure (now in the Hungarian National Museum in Budapest) represents a boar, the favorite food at most Celtic feasts. These dinners were lavish affairs that often degenerated into brawls as warriors argued over who should receive the hero's portion.

Cernach of Ulster. Connall claims the right to carve the haunch because he has killed so many of Cet's fellow Connacht men that he has had a fresh head for a pillow every night for a year. That argument impresses even Cet, who acknowledges Connall's right to carve. However, as a parting shot, Cet says, "You would not be the carver if my brother Anluan was here, for he is a greater warrior than I am." Connall laughs and replies that Anluan is indeed present, for, he says, "I killed him this morning and here is his head to prove it!" He then throws the head at Cet with such force that it knocks Cet down. Connall then begins the carving and takes the whole animal, leaving nothing but the knuckles for Cet and his Connacht men. This stinginess, however, proves too great an insult, and the Connacht men spring to their feet and attack the other guests; the feast quickly becomes a bloodbath in which parts of bodies float out the door on rivers of blood.

The argument over the hero's portion was a constant element of Celtic society. Roman, Greek, and early Christian writers report similar incidents during their five hundred years of contact with Celtic groups throughout Europe. War, killing, and violence were the constant trademarks of the Celts. They decorated their homes with the heads of their defeated enemies and preserved the heads of the most famous in honey, keeping them so that they could, when the occasion merited, be taken out and exhibited to honored guests.

However, the same records of the "civilized" Romans, Greeks, and early Christians that recount the violence of Celtic society also present a picture of a people with some very positive attributes. The Celts were not simple raiders of the lands around them. They had a well-developed agricultural economy, created wonders of metallurgy, and built an extensive commercial empire centered in locations that developed into such great modern trading

LEFT: Detail of a gold bracelet found near Lasgraisses, France. According to tradition, this bracelet, now in the Bibliothèque Nationale in Paris, was stolen from the Greek sanctuary of Apollo at Delphi when the temple was raided by the Celts in 279 B.C. The fearsome Celts are said to have fled in terror from Apollo's temple when the god appeared at the head of a ghostly band of Greek warriors.

OPPOSITE: A statue of a Celtic warrior dating from the sixth century B.C. Celtic warriors often went into battle wearing only a gold torque, a conical cap made of metal or leather, and a leather belt. While the sight of male genitals was said to inspire terror in the enemy, there was in fact a medical benefit to be derived from this lack of clothing—wounds could not become infected, as they often did, by cloth fibers getting caught in them. This stone figure, now in the Wuerttembergisches Landesmuseum, Stuttgart, Germany, is from a burial barrow at Hirschlanden, Germany.

centers as Bonn, Trier, Frankfurt, Würzburg, Augsburg, Geneva, Lyons, Toulouse, Verona, Budapest, Belgrade, and Leiden.

The Celts also created their own coinage and traded as equals with the Romans, importing wine and luxury goods while exporting grain, horses, and metallurgical crafts. Gaius Julius Caesar fully expected the wealth of Gaul—once he had captured it—to allow him to compete for control of the Roman world against Marcus Lucinius Crassus (112–53 B.C.), reputed to be the wealthiest man in Rome, and Gnaeus Pompeius Magnus (106–48 B.C.), who had recently stolen the treasury of Mithridates Magnus, one of the richest potentates of the eastern Mediterranean. Caesar was not disappointed—he returned from his eight years of conquest in Gaul with enough money to pay off his 75,000,000-denarii debt and bribe the whole Roman electorate (spending approximately 20,000,000 denarii), with enough left to treat the citizens of Rome to the most expensive gladiatorial combat in the city's history. He did all this with the money he stole from the Gauls, funds that also allowed him to pursue his lavish lifestyle. While there is no way to estimate the actual amount that Caesar took from the Celts in Gaul, it must have been incredible, for he flooded the market with so much gold that its value fell below the value of silver.

Gaul continued to be a wealthy province even after the Roman conquest, and the Romans continued to milk the area for years. According to the Greek historian Dio Cassius, when the mad emperor Caligula (A.D. 12–41, emperor A.D. 37–41) exhausted the Roman treasury in A.D. 39, he immediately set off for Gaul to replenish his finances from its "overwhelming wealth." Another historian of that time, Strabo, writing in A.D. 23, described a shrine at Tolosa (modern Toulouse) in which the Celts stored 100,000 pounds (45,000kg) of gold and 110,000 pounds (49,500kg) of silver.

THE ORIGINS
OF THE CELTS

The Romans, who at the same time were scared, fascinated, and repulsed by the Celts, had their own legends about Celtic beginnings. According to these legends, the Celts were descended from Hercules, who, on his way to steal the Golden Apples of the Hesperidae and the Cattle of Geryon—two of his famous twelve labors—paused often on his journey to mate with various local princesses. The true origins of the Celts are unfortunately not so titillating.

The Celts did not emerge as a distinct group until 800 B.C. Before that, their ances-tors were an indistinguishable part of the swarm in central Europe. Linguists, however, have built a theory about their origins that leads from the Russian steppes, through several migrations, to their first firm date in the ninth century B.C.

About 3000 B.C., a group of people whose language, called Old European, would some-day evolve into Sanskrit, Iranian, Hittite, and Hellenic, which would in turn evolve into Indian, Persian, Greek, Latin, Welsh, and Gaelic, lived in the area of what is now Russia where the Volga River empties into the Caspian Sea. Archaeologists who deal with tangi-ble objects such as pots, spear points, and bones, instead of vocabulary and syntax, call these people the Kurgan culture. *Kurgan* is Russian for "mound," specifically the burial mounds that these Volga dwellers built for their high-ranking dead.

By 2400 B.C. the Kurgan people had do-mesticated horses and learned to make bronze weapons and beautiful jewelry of gold, silver, and turquoise; they had also started to mi-grate to the west and south. By 2000 B.C. one branch, which archaeologists now call the Indo-Europeans, had moved into the area that is now Turkey. By 1600 B.C. they were recog-nizable as the Hittites. Another branch of these people had begun to filter into Greece at about the same time, eventually becoming the Mycenaeans, while still another group—the one of interest to us—had by this time en-tered the lower Danube River Valley. There Danubian invaders, called by archaeologists the Corded Ware People or the Battle Ax People, slowly continued their move to the west and north into the areas that today are Denmark, Sweden, Norway, Britain, and Bohemia. By 1200 B.C. they were firmly set-tled, but sometime around 1000 B.C. they re-ceived some unwelcome attention from the Scythians, another group from the Russian steppes. The Scythians gave to the people who

The Celts at one time dominated all of western Europe, with the exception of Scandinavia. By the first century B.C., however, they had begun moving north and west toward the British Isles because of attacks by Germans and Romans. Today the Celtic population of Europe is largely confined to Wales, Cornwall, Brittany, and the western edge of Scotland.

would someday evolve into the Celts an artistic addiction to fantastic, stylized animal forms, plus innovative ideas in horse paraphernalia, like snaffles and reins. These last elements allowed a man to maneuver and control a horse more easily, thereby improving mobility and the ability to fight on horseback. The Scythians also gave to these "Proto-Celts" the custom of taking heads as war trophies, as well as the grooming customs of combing the hair of the head straight up and stiffening it with lime into a kind of cockscomb, wearing mustaches, and strutting around in brightly colored, checkered plaids.

By 800 B.C. a culture that most scholars and archaeologists agree was Celtic was flourishing north of the Alps all the way to the Baltic and Atlantic shores. Historians and ar-

chaeologists, whose audiences demand neat names and dates, have chosen to call this earliest Celtic culture Hallstatt, after an especially rich archaeological site in Austria. The same people have determined that the Hallstatt culture flourished between 800 and 600 B.C.

This site was discovered in 1846 by an Austrian civil servant, Georg Ramsauer, in the little Austrian town of Hallstatt. Hallstätters had been mining salt from beneath the local mountain for thousands of years and burying their dead in neat mounds on that same mountain for an equally long time. On his own initiative, Ramsauer had begun excavating those graves, and he eventually convinced the Austro-Hungarian government to take up the task. There were 2,500 graves in all, and it was these graves that provided the world with its first good view of the early Celts. The grave goods—sword hilts, fibulae (large, highly decorated safety pins designed to hold cloaks around the shoulders), and numerous bronze castings of animals—have given the world an art style known as Hallstatt. This style, which between 800 and 600 B.C. was found all over western Europe from Ireland to Spain to Hungary, combines elements from Scythian, Roman, Greek, and Etruscan art. Stylized animals, ornate whorls, and geometric designs predominate. There is a feeling for design and proportion, but little concern for accurate representation of animal or human forms. One feels that the Hallstatt artists could certainly have portrayed anything in absolutely accurate detail, but preferred to experiment with design and shape for the fun of it.

Probably the most dramatic collection of Hallstatt art comes from the tomb of a Celtic princess, a woman whose name is lost but whom art historians have chosen to call the Princess of Vix, after the modern French village near where she was found. The site is six hundred miles (960km) from Hallstatt and is near the source of the Seine River (called the Sequona River in Celtic), on the slopes of Mont Lassois, where in the seventh century B.C. a Celtic fortress sat across a trade route that ran between the English Channel and the Rhône River. The treasures from the tomb, which are now in a museum at nearby Châtillon-sur-Seine, are rich and varied. They include a golden crown adorned with stylized Scythian horses, bronze bowls of exacting workmanship, Attic black-figured pottery imported from Greece, and Etruscan pitchers and bowls. The prize of the museum is an immense bronze krater (a bowl for mixing wine and water) thirteen feet (4m) in circumference, five feet (1.5m) high, and weighing 460 pounds (207kg). In the ancient world, wine was seldom drunk in its unadulterated form—people were astounded, for instance,

when Alexander the Great drank his wine "neat." The krater was manufactured south of the Alps, probably in Singidunum (modern Belgrade), by Greeks anxious to win the favor of the Celts, who controlled the movement of tin and iron into the Mediterranean Basin. The krater was a rich gift; clearly somebody from the south felt that the Celts were people whose favor was worth cultivating.

The Hallstatt culture, however, was merely one stage in the development of the Celtic culture. By 600 B.C. Europe north of the Alps was dominated by hundreds of Celtic *oppida*, fortified cities that controlled trade routes. From 600 B.C. until nearly the beginning of the Christian era, the Celtic world was

This bronze representation of a goat, which dates from about 300 B.C. and is now in the Moravian Museum in Brno, Czech Republic, was once affixed to the side of a wooden pitcher.

typified by the La Tene culture, which was vastly more sophisticated and developed than the Hallstatt.

The La Tene culture takes its name from a site in northern Switzerland on the shores of Lake Neuchâtel. Archaeological investigation between 1880 and 1885 and again between 1907 and 1917 revealed a store of weapons, tools, utensils, and other artifacts so distinctive and so much more developed than the earlier Hallstatt material that when scholars found similar material throughout Europe they concluded that La Tene typified a whole era of Celtic culture. The material remains were so rich and so developed that they undoubtedly pointed to a massive Celtic rela-

tionship—economic and otherwise—with the Roman and Greek cultures to the south. The Celts of the time undoubtedly profited from this trade, and some became quite wealthy.

It is from the La Tene period that the most impressive monuments of Celtic art come. The Basse-Yutz flagons, the Battersea and Witham shields, with their coral and enamel rondels, the numerous helmets, the famous Gundestrup Cauldron, and other artistic treasures are the justly famous artifacts of this period. Furthermore, examples of La Tene continued to be produced in Ireland long after the Celts on the European mainland were defeated by the Romans and absorbed into that empire. Because Ireland was

This reconstruction of a Celtic house of the La Tene period (600–200 B.C.) is part of a reconstructed Celtic village near Asparn/Zara, Austria. Although the Romans considered the Celts barbarians, they were nonetheless impressed by the cleanliness of Celtic towns and of the Celts themselves.

The most famous artifact of Celtic Europe is the Gundestrup Cauldron, which was found in a bog in Gundestrup, Denmark, in 1891. This cauldron, which was probably created in northern Greece about 100 B.C., is made out of gilded silver and measures over 29 inches (73cm) in diameter. The outside surface of the cauldron displays portraits of seven Celtic gods, and the inside bears a representation of a ritual procession (see page 26). On the bottom of the cauldron is the figure of a bull (see page 51). This artifact was purposely broken up and sunk in a bog as an offering to a god.

isolated from the rest of Europe, Irish art continued the traditions of Celtic art and ornamentation well into the Christian era. The Ardagh Chalice, the Crozier of Clonmacnoise, the Tara Brooch, and of course the beautiful illuminated manuscripts such as *The Book of Durrow*, *The Book of Kells*, and the *Lindisfarne Gospels*, which were created well after the beginning of the Christian era, all show the ornamental magnificence of La Tene culture.

This magnificence is the artistic counterpart to a burst of geographic expansion throughout the whole Celtic world that was a result of a revolution in Celtic technology. Around 600 B.C., Celtic smiths learned how to make cheap, but durable, iron tools and weapons. In the earlier Hallstatt period, iron had been difficult to produce and had been used primarily for weapons. Now, however, everyday tools could be made of iron, including massive wheeled plows that could break

new, previously unplanted soils in northern Europe. This expansion of farmland resulted in more food and a larger population. That, in turn, often created an opportunity for political expansion, and it is no coincidence that during the La Tene period many small Celtic settlements grew into large towns as new, energetic chieftains struggled to build their empires, accumulating in the process gold and silver as well as the symbols of wealth and power that are made from these metals.

It is also no coincidence that this was the period during which the Celts first spilled over into the Greco-Roman world and challenged the people of those cultures for control of the north shore of the Mediterranean. In 386 B.C. the Celts sacked Rome; in 335 B.C. they clashed with the Macedonian army of Alexander the Great; by 279 B.C. they had moved on to destroy the temples of the Greek gods at Delphi; and by 276 B.C. they were in

The beginning page of
the Gospel of Mark as
found in *The Book of
Durrow*, which dates
from about A.D. 650
and is now stored
at Trinity College,
Dublin, Ireland.
Although this book
is from an earlier era
than *The Book of Kells*
(see page 11), it also
shows the characteris-
tic Celtic style. The
famous Celtic spiral
designs, called the
"Trumpet Pattern"
by historians, are
clearly visible in the
design of the first two
letters in INITIUM
EVANGELII IHN XPI
("The Beginning
of the Gospel of
Jesus Christ"). The
"Trumpet Pattern"
is also found on
artifacts from
Hallstatt, Austria,
that date from
1,200 years before
The Book of Durrow.

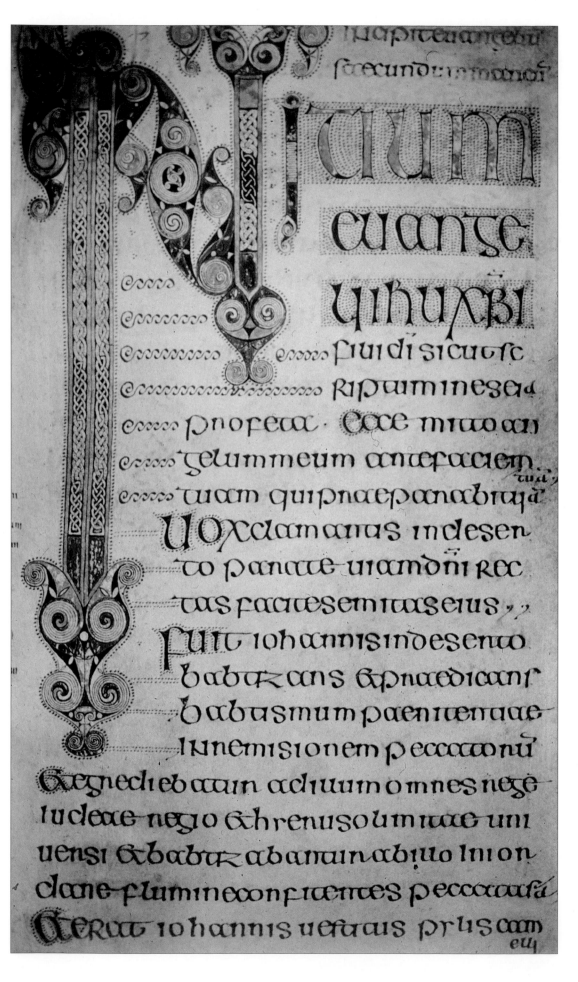

central Anatolia (modern Turkey), where they founded the kingdom of Galatia. In A.D. 55, after about three hundred years—a period of time during which the Galatian Celts "settled down" and became "civilized"—Saint Paul introduced the Galatian Celts to Christianity.

THE CELTIC MENACE: A ROMAN PERSPECTIVE

If there is one thing the authors of the ancient sources agree on, it is that the Celts were Rome's worst nightmare for over three hundred years. Titus Livius, Gaius Julius Caesar (who, besides being the architect of the Roman empire, was also an accomplished historian), and Marcus Annaeus Lucan, who all wrote about the Celts, pay tribute to their courage and their deep religious feeling, but also stress their barbarism and brutality.

Of all the peoples Rome fought in her long history, only the Celts were able to extract a bribe as the price of peace from the Romans. In 391 B.C., a group of Celts, hungry for land, came over the Alps and down into the Po River Valley. Five years later, a Celtic chieftain named Brennus attacked a Roman army near the Allia River and destroyed it; even worse than the defeat itself was the apparent cause—it seems that this Celtic victory was due more to Roman cowardice than to superior strategy on the part of the Celts. The Romans were so shaken by the defeat that they did not try another attack on the Celts in the open, but retreated up into the Capitoline fortress in Rome itself. The defeated soldiers did not pause to close the city gates, and they even abandoned their older citizens to the enemy.

When the Celts entered the city, they discovered the oldest, most distinguished members of the Roman Senate sitting calmly outside their homes, apparently too proud to follow the safest course of action (which to them seemed cowardly): running. When one of the Celtic warriors tugged at the beard of Senator Marcus Papirius, the Roman official struck him on the head with his senatorial staff. This action precipitated a wholesale massacre, and the Celts burned the entire city to the ground. To this day, when archaeologists excavate sites in Rome, they can find a thick layer of ash that separates the city of Rome as it existed before the invasion from the city built afterward.

The eastern side of the Cross of the Scriptures at Clonmacnoise, Ireland. Dozens of these stone crosses, which are usually over seven feet (2.1m) tall and decorated with interlaced Celtic designs surrounding depictions of events in Christ's life, can be found throughout Ireland. At the center of this cross is a figure of Christ wearing a crown and holding a cross.

Celtic warriors, under the direction of a Druid, dedicate their weapons to war against the Romans. In the fourth century B.C., the Celts attempted to subdue what is now Italy and share in the wealth of the Roman and Greek inhabitants. The sack of Rome by the Celts in 386 B.C. created in the Romans a hatred of all things Celtic, and the Roman legions led by Gaius Julius Caesar decisively defeated the Celts in 52 B.C.

Unable to beat the Celts, the Romans agreed to pay a ransom of 1,000 pounds (450kg) of gold. When the Romans objected to the scale the Celts used to measure the gold, Brennus, the Celtic leader, threw his huge sword onto the scale to further unbalance the weight and snarled at the Romans, "*Vae victis!*" ("Woe to the vanquished!") The Romans saw his point, made the required payment, and from that time regarded the Celts as brutes from hell.

From then on, the Romans and the Celts fought often. In 298 B.C. and again in 285 B.C. the Romans defeated the Celts, in the latter battle exterminating an entire tribe, the Senones. Sixty-nine years later, the Celts allied themselves with Hannibal and the Carthaginians and helped rout three Roman armies. In 113 B.C. the Cimbri, a Celtic tribe, invaded Italy once more and in four years crushed four Roman armies. The Romans began to believe that the giants from the north were invincible. Only the brilliant tactics of Gaius Marius saved the Italian peninsula from becoming a Celtic province. It is no wonder, then, that Roman writers painted such a harsh picture of the Celts.

The Roman historians Gaius Julius Caesar and Marcus Annaeus Lucan and the Greek writers Strabo and Diodorus Siculius all accuse the Celts of hideous practices. Caesar, who wrote for a Roman audience that glorified their status as free men, emphasized that the Celts lived in a world dominated by tyrants who controlled the Celtic masses in a master-slave relationship. Diodorus, playing upon the sexual mores of his Roman readers, asserted that the Celts were notorious homosexuals who avoided the embraces of women and performed sexual perversions in groups of three; this was especially perverse, according to Diodorus, because Celtic women were tall and blond, features the dark Italians practically worshiped.

In religious matters, these writers presented the Celts at their absolute worst. The Romans were fascinated with the Druids, the priestly class of the Celts. Caesar asserted that the Druids were a Europe-wide group with common beliefs and an established series of schools for teaching those beliefs. These Druids, Caesar wrote, presided over all of Celtic society, making legal decisions, predicting the future, and placating the gods. Their temples, according to Lucan, were found in dark and gloomy clearings in the midst of oak groves. The oak trees were carved into grotesque shapes and the clearings were piled high with "hideous offerings" (presumably human limbs); also, the oak trees were regularly sprinkled with human blood. The ground in the groves frequently shook, mysterious groans emanated from the area, and snakes slithered through the roots of the trees. So ghastly were these places that birds refused to perch in the surrounding trees and even the Druid priests dared not enter except at certain times of the day when the terrible gods of the Celts were believed to be absent. In his account, Caesar wrote that these sacred groves were the sites of horrible sacrifices where

A Victorian-era representation of a grove where Druids placated the fierce Celtic gods. Such places were usually dominated by sacred stones and oaks, and were regarded with such terror that even the Druids who presided over them feared to enter after sunset.

This representation from the inside of the Gundestrup Cauldron (see page 21) shows a religious ceremony and procession in which a priest or god seems to be plunging a victim head-first into a cauldron. According to some scholars, the figure being dipped into the cauldron may not be a victim at all, but the lucky recipient of a second lease on life. Magical life-giving cauldrons are an important feature of many Celtic myths. The members of the procession include warriors carrying shields and wearing helmets, horsemen with animal crests on their helmets, and a group of musicians playing ram-headed trumpets.

people were forced into huge human-shaped wicker cages that were then set on fire. Supposedly, condemned criminals were the usual victims, but if the supply of felons was inadequate, innocents were also used. So fearsome were the Druidic sites that Caesar's soldiers, tough legionnaires that they were, refused to enter one such place near Marseilles until Caesar entered first.

Roman writers also stated that the Celts took the heads of enemies slain in battle or during raids and decorated their homes with them, held funerals during which wives and slaves were burned alongside the corpse, and enforced their laws through torture and mutilation. In one source it is claimed that sacrificial victims were stuck head-first into huge cauldrons and drowned. Certainly there seems to be a representation of just such an event on the side of the Gundestrup Cauldron. Knowing this, it is not hard to imagine the great cauldron from Vix, France, also being used for just such a purpose.

Were such atrocities actually practiced? If so, were they truly as common in the Celtic culture as these writers claimed? We must re-

member that most of these grisly accounts were written by the Romans, who had fought the Celts for centuries—often with disastrous results. Stories like these are just the kind to inspire fellow Romans to resist a dangerous foe. Since the Celts left no written records of their own, it is questionable how far we should trust these hostile sources—the best we can say about such stories is "perhaps."

THE CONTINENTAL MYTHS: WHAT HAS BEEN LOST

Even though the Celts dominated Europe for nearly a millennium, we know very little about their mythology, quite simply because so little of it has survived. On the one hand, the mythology of the continental Celts died out after the Roman conquest, as the Celtic culture became Romanized; on the other hand, the Celtic mythology of that part of

ligunt pfenniam roncā. Cafem chonam meretur
a pso beacorum apfox chonicralem retribucione re
cipium p corrupabilibus.

Almost all of what
we know of Celtic
mythology comes to
us secondhand
through Christian
monks who copied the
myths from local
filids, or storytellers.
It seems likely
that these Christian
brothers "sanitized"
the myths as they
wrote them down.
Here a monk sits at
his desk under an oil
lamp, illustrating
a manuscript.

they refer to. But there is no way to know, for the myths themselves are lost. What gruesome tale is represented by the so-called Monster of Noves, France, whose jaws hold the head of a man and whose claws rest on the tops of two human heads? What delightful story is concealed in the tiny bronze statue of what may be a goddess offering a bear a basket of fruit? Barring the unlikely discovery of a previously unknown Druidic holy book, we will probably never know. Historians are able to piece together only the barest outlines of the Celtic pantheon.

At the top of the Celtic divinity heap is the god Lugh, whose widespread appeal can be inferred from the names of various modern European cities that seem to have been derived from his name: Lyons, Laon, Leiden, Leignitz. According to several Roman writers, his feast day, which seems to have been August 1, was called Lugnasad. His sacred symbol was the spear and he was always accompanied by ravens. In some representations he is shown with only one eye. The spear, raven, and single eye are also attributes of the Germanic god Wotan, and it is certain that the Germans grafted aspects of Lugh onto their chief god. The Irish also had a god named Lugh, whom the Christian monks converted into a sort of super-hero who excelled in every art and defeated his enemies with a magic spear.

Another god of the continental Celts was Teutates, a god who reveled in sacrifices of human victims drowned in cauldrons. Caesar, whose statements about such things are no more reliable than those of other Roman writers, claimed that Teutates was given credit for inventing all the crafts of mankind. In statues and stone reliefs of Teutates, he is depicted wearing a long, flowing mustache and sideburns. The Gundestrup Cauldron shows a figure that meets this description holding two stags by their hind legs. Whatever legend this

Europe the Romans did not conquer—Ireland and Wales—survived only after passing through the sieve of Christian scribes who wrote down these tales but sometimes removed "offensive" pagan elements.

At one time there must have been a rich mythology surrounding the Celtic people of continental Europe, for the names of hundreds of deities survive in inscriptions and place names. Surviving archaeological treasures, such as the Gundestrup Cauldron, and sculptured pieces show Celtic deities in what one can only assume are representations of various myths. It is maddening to realize that the details of these myths will never be known. The Gundestrup Cauldron, for instance, preserves a picture of a being commonly believed to be Cernunnos, the Celtic god of the dead, who is shown holding a snake in one hand and a torque, or collar, in the other; he has antlers and is sitting in the midst of wolves and reindeer. On the other side of the cauldron, a female figure wearing a short skirt dances with what looks like a dog. We would like to know what these figures represent, what story out of Celtic mythology

RIGHT: The god Lugh, a dominant figure in many legends of Celtic Ireland, may have been a god of light. His annual festival, which was called Lugnasad, was held on August 1 of every year. Lugh was not only a warrior, but also a mighty sorcerer and the master of all human crafts. Representations of Lugh usually show him accompanied by two ravens, birds who acted as both messengers and spies.

FAR RIGHT: When archaeologists excavated the basement of Notre Dame in Paris, they discovered stone sculptures of Celtic deities, thus proving that the site was originally a sacred spot for the Celts. One sculpture was of a three-horned bull, a Celtic symbol of virility and good luck. More than forty representations of three-horned bulls have been found in Europe. The figure shown here is now in the Musée de Cluny et des Thèrmes, Paris.

refers to is lost, yet the importance of Teutates to Celtic culture can be inferred from the fact that one of the most powerful tribes the Romans fought—the Teutons—took their name from his.

About the rest of the Celtic gods we know tantalizingly little, and no stories like those that make classical mythology so appealing survive on the Continent. Among these little-known deities is Esus, whose role in the Celtic pantheon is not clear although representations of him appear all over Europe. His sacred animal was the bull, and in some relief sculptures he is identified with cranes. He enjoyed human sacrifice, and those killed in his name were suspended from trees to die. Esus' relationship to trees, albeit with somewhat different implications, is illustrated in two reliefs—one found under Notre Dame in Paris and another from Trier, Germany, portray him cutting down trees.

Cernunnos, the Celtic god of the underworld, was also a deity of much importance.

He is almost always depicted wearing reindeer antlers, and is usually shown in close proximity to animals. Sometimes he is pictured holding a bag of money—assumed by some to be a sign of fertility, although it seems peculiar to have a god who functions as both a deity of fertility and a god of death. His special day, which was called Samhain by the Celts, was November 1; this holiday is the origin of our Halloween. His horns and his association with the underworld tempted some early Christians to identify him with Satan, but there is absolutely nothing to associate him with evil; rather, he seemed to function not only as god of the underworld but also as a god of plenty. In Rome there survives one monument to him, dedicated by French sailors, that gives the impression that he was a god of the common man.

There is only one goddess about whom historians know anything more than the barest details: the goddess Sulevia, or Sulis, who in Britain was also called Brigantia. When the Romans learned of this goddess, they identified her with their own Minerva. Sulevia was believed to preside over sacred,

healing springs, such as the one at Bath, England, which were called by the Romans *Aquae Sulis*, "the Waters of Sulis." Along with a male companion deity named Maponos, Sulevia was said to have provided miraculous cures. Numerous springs dedicated to these two deities can be found in western Europe, and archaeologists have recovered from these springs hundreds of wooden carvings that seem to represent afflicted parts of the human body. These figures have led scholars to believe that it was customary for people coming to the spring in search of a cure to offer the goddess a symbol of the illness. A similar custom survives today in the American Southwest, where some Hispanic Americans leave pewter representations of afflicted body parts called *malegros* at certain shrines that are sup-

posed to be places of healing. As Brigantia, the goddess was adopted by the early Christian missionaries to Ireland as Saint Brighid, and the springs that had been sacred to Brigantia became sacred to Saint Brighid. There is, for instance, a spring sacred to Brighid near Fouchart, Ireland, and another at Llyn Cerrig Bach on the island of Anglesey in the Irish Sea, both of which were once sacred to Brigantia. The goddess and the saint share the same sacred day, February 1, and Saint Brighid's shrine at Kildare, Ireland, is built over an earlier shrine to Sulevia.

Unfortunately, the knowledge we have of other Celtic mythological beings from mainland Europe consists mostly of a list of names with next to no personal attributes or surviving mythology. Ogmios, whose surviving

One of the depictions on the Gundestrup Cauldron (see page 21) is of the god Cernunnos, who is pictured wearing antlers and holding a torque in one hand and a ram-headed snake in the other. The snake, which appears in representations of Cernunnos throughout Europe, may represent virility. On several other monuments Cernunnos holds an open bag from which coins or grain spill out. This suggests his possible role as a god of bounty.

monuments depict an old man carrying a club, was apparently a Celtic version of the Greek hero Hercules. But unlike Hercules, who was exceptionally stupid, Ogmios was depicted as wise—it was Ogmios, according to the Greek historian Lucan of Samosata, writing in about A.D. 150, who invented *ogham*, the system of writing developed by the Celts. Another deity was Epona, the goddess of horses, who is known from numerous European sites. She is usually depicted sitting sidesaddle, and there are often sheep in the representation; this combination of sheep and horse obviously refers to some now lost myth. In some sculptures, she is seen with a male figure behind her, which has been interpreted by some as a representation of Epona leading the souls of the dead to the realm of Cernunnos. Belenus was a healing god often identified with the Greek god Apollo. Belenus is associated by the Roman poet Decimus Magnus

Ausonius (C. A.D. 310–395) with a number of healing temples in Aquitania. He is also associated with the sun, not as a sun god per se, but in reference to the healing aspects of the sun. Sucellos, the god of alcoholic beverages, was apparently popular, to judge from the numerous representations scattered throughout western Europe that depict him carrying a small beer barrel suspended from a pole; he is often shown carrying a hammer, but the significance of this is unknown.

The frustration Celtic scholars experience due to their lack of knowledge about the Celtic pantheon is compounded by the fact that many of Europe's rivers are named for Celtic deities about whom nothing is known—the goddess Sequona gave her name to the Seine, the goddess Matrona to the Marne, and Souconna to the Sâone. Certainly it is unfortunate that such a rich mythological heritage has been lost.

CHAPTER

II

THE
IRISH MYTHS

hile much has been lost, a great deal of Celtic mythology survives—albeit in a somewhat corrupted form—in the mythology of Ireland, which begins, logically enough, with the peopling of the Emerald Isle. These "origin myths" are preserved in a twelfth-century manuscript written by Christian monks entitled *The Book of the Conquest of Ireland*, which is usually referred to simply as *The Book of Invasions* (*Leabhar Gabhala* in Irish Gaelic). It is important to remember that dozens of Irish myths survive only

---

With the coming of the Christians, Celtic society was thrown into disarray and its hierarchy disrupted. Because of this, Irish *filids* such as this one often found themselves in dire straits—the audience for their stories was greatly reduced.

33

because Christian monks decided to preserve these pagan myths by writing them down. Throughout the rest of Europe, the Christian community had decided to ignore pagan mythology, and most of it has therefore been lost. Irish Christian scribes sometimes recast these myths to take out the most blatant pagan references, but they usually let most of them remain. They apparently wrote down the myths more or less exactly as they heard them from the *filids*, the Irish storytellers. Indeed, some of the earliest Irish converts may have been filids, for such men associated with the Irish nobility, and we know that throughout Europe conversion to Christianity began with the rulers.

The one concession these early Christian copyists did make to their faith was to change the Irish gods from deities to heroic men and women with superhuman powers. Lugh, for instance, who was certainly a god on the Continent, is portrayed in *The Book of Invasions* as a human who is immensely strong, large, and clever.

THE PEOPLING
OF IRELAND

It was undoubtedly a Christian who recorded in *The Book of Invasions* that the original settlers of Ireland were fifty women and three men led by Cesair, a granddaughter of Noah. Unfortunately, the flood that Noah survived killed all of these early Irish except one man named Fintan, who used magic to change himself into a salmon, thus surviving the flood. When the flood ended, he changed himself into a hawk and flew over the land watching the Irish countryside reemerge from the receding waters. For years Fintan lived in Ireland alone except for the evil Formorians, a dreadful wraithlike race from the north

who were more shadow than substance. They hated humans, but ignored Fintan because of his animal disguise.

The next group to come to Ireland came from Greece. They were led by Partholon, who was accompanied by his wife, Delgnat, noted for both her beauty and her lustfulness; their three sons and their wives; three druids named Tath, Fiss, and Forhmarc; and several hundred followers. These people made a survey of the whole island and found it covered by thick forests with only one clear plain in the center. Ireland at this time had only three lakes and nine rivers. Partholon and his people cut down enough trees to create four more plains, thus providing space for farming. They then invented brewing and introduced laws governing the ownership of land.

Throughout their stay, these immigrants fought constantly with the Formorians, who were led by the brutal Cicul. But the Formorians were not Partholon's only problem, for soon after the invention of brewing he discovered he was a cuckold—his beautiful wife was sleeping with his servant Topa, and the two adulterers were compounding their crime by drinking from the royal beer vat. Partholon decided to set a trap and catch them redhanded. He told his wife he was leaving on an inspection tour, then unexpectedly returned to discover the two in bed. He could have killed them both then and there, but he instead brought them into court for trial. Topa had little to say, but Delgnat defended herself by accusing Partholon of dereliction in his husbandly duties. He had been so busy organizing Ireland, she contended, that he had neglected the bedroom and she, being young and lusty, had let her natural drives rule her actions. The court ruled that while Delgnat was guilty of lustfulness, Partholon was the cause of it and was therefore equally guilty. With this, the two were reconciled and Partholon promised to spend more time at home.

Unfortunately, the royal couple did not have much time to enjoy their new resolve, for soon thereafter a plague came to Ireland and every Greek immigrant died save one man named Tuan, who fled to the mountains, where he lived alone for twenty years.

At the end of this time, Tuan saw a new group of invaders arrive: the Nemedians, so named for their leader, Nemed. The Nemedians were the remnants of a once-mighty fleet that had sailed from some unknown land. Originally, thirty-two ships carrying 560 passengers had sailed, but only one vessel and nine people had survived. Nevertheless, these followers of Nemed did well in Ireland. They and their descendants cut down more timber and created a dozen new plains on which to grow their crops. It was Nemed who built the first palace at a place that would later be called Emhain Macha.

Unfortunately, the Nemedians soon found themselves in conflict with the Formorians, and the two groups fought four titanic battles. As long as Nemed lived, his followers were victorious in these battles, but after he died, the Formorians conquered the Nemedians and extracted tribute every November 1, the Feast of Samhain. The tribute consisted of two-thirds of the Nemedian children born the previous year, plus an equal proportion of their crops and milk. After the Nemedians had lived under this system for several years, they rebelled and came close to defeating their masters. The Formorians were driven back to their most northern fortress, on the island of Tory off the northern coast of Ireland. There the Nemedian hero Ferghus and all but thirty of his followers died fighting the enemy. Some of these people fled Ireland under their new king, Britan, and settled on the island to the east, which was subsequently named Britain. Some, however, went on to Greece, where they sought reinforcements to take back to their Irish homeland.

When this remnant returned to Ireland it was with three new groups of people: the Fir Bolg, the Gailion, and the Fir Dhomhnann. Linguists claim that the Fir Bolg may have been related to the people who later settled Belgium (the Belgae) and that the Fir Dhomhnann may have been the ancestors of the historic Dumnonii of Cornwall. It is possible, therefore, that the Fir Bolg were real people and that their story is an example of a crossroads at which myth and historical fact meet.

The Fir Bolg soon dominated the new arrivals, becoming the ruling group. As rulers, they made a number of important changes. They divided the country into five sections: Ulster, Leinster, Munster, Connacht, and Meath. They also instituted the idea of kingship and imparted to it a sacred character.

Their most famous ruler was Eochy mac Erc, whom myth credits with writing the first complete legal code for Ireland. He also stood in such favor with the gods that Ireland enjoyed a plentiful harvest in every year of his reign. Happiness and prosperity were further guaranteed in that during his rule no rain fell in Ireland and only the morning and evening dew was necessary to water the crops. No rain at all may seem a strange symbol of well-being to most modern people unless they have suffered through the constant dampness of Ireland—the green of the Emerald Isle is charming, but at a price. To his further credit, Eochy mac Erc seems to have concluded a peace with the Formorians, something none of the other mythical settlers of Ireland seems to have been able to do.

This happy state of affairs did not last, however, for soon another group of immigrants arrived in Ireland. These were the descendants of those same Nemedians who had fled to Britain after their defeat by the Formorians. While in Britain, these people had acquired powers far above those of mere mortals. They had become, in short, demigods, with physical and magical powers far beyond those of the Fir Bolg, who—according to the myths—watched dumbfounded one May morning as these powerful newcomers appeared out of the sky and floated gently down to earth.

These magical beings were called the Tuatha de Danu, the "People of the Goddess Danu." They may be the mythical reflection of an historic invasion of Ireland in about 500 B.C. of people who brought with them the secret of ironworking. The myths concerning the Tuatha record not only their skill with iron but also their successes in medicine and the composition of poetry.

Immediately upon their arrival the Tuatha de Danu fell into conflict with both the Fir Bolg and the Formorians. After a great

battle at a site called Magh Tuiredh on the western coast, where with their iron weapons they defeated the Fir Bolg and with their magic powers they defeated the Formorians, the Tuatha de Danu drove the former into Connacht and concluded an armed truce with the latter. The victory at Magh Tuiredh was due to three magical tools that the Tuatha brought with them to Ireland: the spear of Lugh, which unerringly found its mark; the sword of Nuadha, which always drew blood; and the great cauldron of the Daghda, which

OPPOSITE: According to legend, Ireland has been troubled by fearsome creatures from the time of its settling. Shown here are the Formorians.

BELOW: The Fir Bolg, a legendary group of invaders from Britain, were the first to divide Ireland into five kingdoms: Ulster, Leinster, Munster, Connacht (or Connaught), and Meath.

IRELAND
just before
THE ENGLISH INVASION

Scale of English Miles

always remained full of Irish porridge no matter how much was taken out of it. According to some archaeologists, a more realistic appraisal of their victory is that the utilization by the Tuatha of lightweight, finely made iron spears enabled them to overcome the Fir Bolg, whose weapons were much more cumbersome. Perhaps the Fir Bolg were armed with flint or copper weapons—no match for weapons of iron.

Whatever the reason for victory, the Tuatha paid a heavy price for it—the dead of both sides were said to litter the ground more thickly than snowflakes, and the mighty Tuatha king, Nuadha, had his hand cut off and thus became ineligible to be king, as Tuatha law specifically demanded a whole man for the job. Nuadha stepped down and, in an attempt at reconciliation, the Tuatha offered their throne to Bress, whose father was a Formorian named Elatha and whose mother was a Tuatha princess.

Bress' rule soon became oppressive and the Tuatha found themselves paying heavy tribute to the Formorians and building new fortifications for them. In addition, Bress proved to be a stingy ruler, for he refused to entertain visiting Tuatha chieftains in the accepted style—when they visited his palace, they did not leave with knives covered with grease or breath smelling of beer. Soon the niggardliness of Bress became known to the whole country and was satirized by the bard Coirbre so harshly that Bress broke out in a hideous rash that was considered as disfiguring as Nuadha's missing hand. Bress refused to vacate the throne, however, and the Tuatha began secretly to gather weapons and hone their magic for yet another battle.

The preparations for this new war took seven years, and during this period the powers of the exiled Nuadha were restored by the Druid-physician Cian, who fashioned for Nuadha a new hand of silver that functioned

DRAVN

better than a real one. Because of this prosthetic, Nuadha was able to reclaim his position as the rightful king of the Tuatha. Oddly enough, he did not remain king for long, for there soon arrived at Tara (Nuadha's capital) a new hero who assumed the kingship and led the Tuatha to victory.

The name of this new king was Lugh. His father was the Druid Cian and his mother was Eithne, a daughter of King Balor of the Formorians. Lugh had been raised by his uncle, a blacksmith who had concealed the boy's identity in those unsettled times. (Lugh's identity had been concealed also because his grandfather Balor had heard a prophecy that

When the Tuatha de Danu, led by King Nuadha (third figure from right), and the mortal Irish settlers were preparing for war with the Formorians, the great warrior-king Lugh (third from left) came to offer them his help. Lugh, however, came to them dressed in clothing ill befitting his station, and the chieftains consequently were reluctant to accept him. In this illustration of this pivotal event, King Nuadha raises his silver hand (which was fashioned for him by Lugh's father, the Druid-physician Cian) to prevent an Irish chieftain from killing Lugh.

he would be killed by one of his grandsons and had consequently sought to murder all possible candidates.) When Lugh reached manhood, the uncle told him of his heritage and sent him to seek his fortune at the court of King Nuadha.

At Tara, Lugh had some difficulty gaining entrance because the gatekeeper had stated that the young man must have a specific skill of value to the court in order to be admitted. Lugh asked if they had a goldsmith at court, and the gatekeeper said yes. Did they have a carpenter? Again the gatekeeper said yes. Perhaps there was need for a musician? No, they already had one. Well then, did they need a poet, a Druid, a scholar, a warrior, or a blacksmith? To each the gatekeeper replied that the court had one or, in some cases, several. Finally, Lugh asked if they had any single person who was skilled in all these arts and crafts, because if they did not, then, he, Lugh, could do all these things and more. Impressed, the gatekeeper let him in.

When Lugh marched into the king's hall, his noble bearing so impressed King Nuadha that he immediately stepped down from his throne and offered it to the young prince. Lugh was joyfully reunited with his father, Cian, and immediately got down to the business of preparing for the coming fight with

Aerial view of Tara, County Meath, Ireland. Tara was the legendary capital of the Tuatha de Danu under King Nuadha the Silver Hand. Tara remained the seat of the high king of Ireland until the English conquest of the island. There has been a settlement at Tara since 2,000 B.C. At the top of the hill on the left is the famous Stone of Fah, which, according to myth, will cry aloud when a true king touches it.

the Formorians. He not only supervised the construction of wonderful weapons, but taught the court Druids incantations to weaken the Formorians by making it impossible for them to urinate. In addition, Lugh and Cian prepared a magic well in which the Tuatha dead could be brought back to life.

Finally, the great day arrived and Lugh led the Tuatha out to battle, which took place on exactly the same site where they had earlier beaten the Fir Bolg—Magh Tuiredh. As is usually the case in mythological battles, the slaughter on both sides was immense. Lugh magically transported himself around the battlefield, lending aid and encouragement wher-

ever the Tuatha troops wavered, and finally came face-to-face with his grandfather, King Balor of the Formorians. Balor possessed a huge, death-dealing eye, the lid of which was so heavy that four men were needed to lift it. Wherever Balor turned this gruesome eye, men died, and the outcome of the entire battle, Lugh realized, hinged on destroying that baneful organ. Lugh gave a mighty shout to attract Balor's attention, and as Balor and his four lid-lifters slowly turned toward Lugh, the young king launched a stone from his sling with such force that it tore through Balor's eye and out the back of his head, killing a dozen Formorians standing behind their king. When

Balor toppled to the ground, the Formorian host fled the field in panic. (In another account of the battle, Balor's horrible eye was pushed out the back of his head by the stone and fell to the ground, where the sight of it killed the Formorian troops standing behind him.)

The Formorians were gathered together and exiled from Ireland forever. Some of them sought to make a private deal with the Tuatha de Danu by promising magic spells that would guarantee four harvests a year, but Lugh rejected this offer and the Formorians departed Ireland for their original homeland to the north.

There was, however, a cloud over the great victory at Magh Tuiredh, for Lugh experienced a vision in which his father, Cian, was killed in the battle. This proved to be true—Cian had been brutally murdered by three Tuatha brothers, Brian, Iuchar, and Iucharba, the sons of Tureinn.

In the collections of Irish myths, the story of the murder of Cian always accompanies the account of the second battle at Magh Tuiredh, even though it has nothing to do with the victory there. To a modern reader, the sudden appearance of the story of Cian's murder and Lugh's vengeance seems to be a violation of the rules of literary organization. To the ancient Irish, however, it would have seemed quite normal, since the great myth cycles were designed to be recited by professional bards who earned their livings by reciting these legends before members of the Irish nobility. The more evenings a bard took in reciting a tale, the longer he enjoyed the hospitality of the noble's home. Therefore a strategic "aside" could prolong a stay at a comfortable stop for an extra day or two.

Lugh had assigned Cian the task of recruiting soldiers in Ulster for the coming bat-

tle. On his way back from this mission Cian was waylaid by the three sons of Tureinn, whose family had long ago sworn vengeance against him for an earlier insult. Realizing his vulnerability, Cian tried to avoid the confrontation by magically changing himself into a pig and joining a nearby herd of swine. Unfortunately for him, however, the eldest son of Tureinn, Brian, saw the change and ran into the midst of the pigs and began spearing them indiscriminately in an attempt to kill the one that was really Cian. Wounded by a spear, Cian asked for time to change back into the shape of a man. The Tureinn brothers agreed, but once the transformation was complete, Cian laughed and said they had been tricked. Now, Cian said, when the murder was discovered the brothers would have to atone for the death of a man, not that of a pig.

At the famous battle of Magh Tuiredh, King Lugh of the Tuatha de Danu saved his army from certain defeat by casting a stone from his sling and putting out the eye of Balor, King of the Formorians. This eye was endowed with powerful magic— Balor was able to kill men with a mere glance. In another version of the story of this battle, Lugh did not put out Balor's eye, but hit him so hard on the back of his head that the Formorian king was turned around to look at the Formorian army, who died when they saw his terrible eye.

One of the sons of Tureinn prepares to kill Cian, the father of Lugh. The Tureinn brothers feared to use their swords to kill Cian lest the weapons leave marks on the corpse that could later be used to identify them.

Enraged by this revelation, the three brothers beat Cian to a pulp with rocks. Apparently, they feared that swords would leave telltale marks specific to each weapon, which might later be used as forensic evidence that could identify them as the killers. When Cian was finally dead, the three danced in the bloody mass, then dug a deep hole, shoved the remains in, and filled the hole with a mound of stones. They then hurried back to Magh Tuiredh to participate in the last skirmishes against the Formorians.

When his father did not return after the battle, Lugh went to search for him. When he passed the spot where the murder had occurred, the rocks covering the corpse cried out at the great injustice of the crime and even identified the killers. Such a declaration by rocks had never before been heard, and Lugh could not doubt the truth of their tale. He returned to Magh Tuiredh and confronted the three brothers. All who heard the tale were horrified and agreed that Lugh should extract any vengeance he chose. At first, Lugh's demands on the brothers appeared so mild that Brian, Iuchar, and Iucharba could not believe their luck. They had merely to gather three

apples, a pigskin, a spear, a war chariot with two fine horses, seven pigs, a hunting dog, and a cooking spit. At the end of all this they had to give three loud shouts from the top of a hill.

The brothers quickly agreed to Lugh's demands, and only then did the king provide with them the details that made the deeds not only arduous but terribly dangerous. The three apples were really the golden apples of the Hesperidae, which when eaten always renewed themselves and could also cure any wound. The pigskin belonged to King Theseus of Greece and could also cure any wound, but, more importantly for the Irish, could change water that was filtered through it into wine. The spear belonged to King Pisear of Persia and had to be kept submerged in water lest it burn down everything within thirty feet of it because of the heat it constantly emitted. The war chariot and its two magical horses belonged to King Dobar of Sicily and could run on water and land, as well as in the air. The seven pigs belonged to King Easel, who lived beyond the Pillars of Hercules; their magical nature was such that no matter how many times they were killed, cooked, and eaten, the next morning they would regenerate completely, thus providing their owners with an inexhaustible source of pork. The dog, which belonged to the King of Ioruaide, never failed to catch what it chased. The cooking spit, which belonged to the women who lived on the undersea island of Fianchuive, imparted to whatever meat was cooked upon it the best flavor in the world. Finally, the hill that the sons of Tureinn were to give three shouts from belonged to King Miodhchaoin, who had sworn that nobody would ever shout from it.

The brothers Tureinn began their tasks, which, despite their evil natures, they performed admirably. The golden apples of the Hesperidae—which classicists will recognize as the same apples that were the subject of Hercules' eleventh labor—lay behind a wall too high to scale, so the brothers changed themselves into hawks and each carried an apple away. To gain the pigskin of King Theseus they masqueraded as bards come to entertain the king; once inside the palace, they grabbed the skin and fought their way out of the startled throng. However, all three were wounded in the fight and so got to test the healing power of the skin immediately after; they poured water through the skin and changed it into an especially good wine that made them drunk for three days. The brothers then used the same bard's disguise with the Persian king and, having gained his confidence, stole his magic spear and used it to fight their way free, splitting the king's head like a melon with one of the three golden apples in the melee.

The acquisition of the chariot and horses required a different tactic. The brothers traveled to Sicily and the court of King Dobar to hire out as mercenary soldiers. Although they performed well and quickly won the respect and trust of King Dobar, they never got to see the chariot or the horses. Finally, they threatened to leave unless they saw the fabled items. The king offered to show the vehicle to his mighty mercenaries and brought it from its

hiding place to drive it around the city and up into the clouds. When King Dobar descended to earth, the brothers clubbed him senseless, jumped into the chariot, and flew away. Celtic myths are full of this kind of heavy-handed resolution. There is seldom the subtlety of the Greek myths where, for instance, when Artemis discovers the hunter Acteon hiding behind a tree with his hounds and watching her bathe, she turns him into a stag and he is slain and eaten by his own dogs.

Next the brothers went beyond the Pillars of Hercules to the realm of King Easel, who was so impressed with the bravery of the three brothers and with their success in accomplishing the first four missions that he simply gave them the seven magical pigs. He even offered to get the great hound of King Ioruaidhe, who happened to be married to his daughter. But even a visit from his father-in-law could not persuade King Ioruaidhe to give up his magic hound, and the brothers were once more reduced to the usual skull-bashing to get their way. The brothers then returned to Ireland to give Lugh the apples, pigskin, spear, chariot, pigs, and hound.

They did not linger at home, however, but immediately continued their quest, confident that they could easily complete the tasks

When the sons of Tureinn cornered Cian, the magician turned himself into a pig and mingled with a herd of swine in an effort to escape. Unfortunately, one of the Tureinn brothers saw the transformation and the brothers killed Cian anyway.

After Lugh
discovered who had
killed his father, he
told the murderers
that he would not
have them killed,
as was his right, but
that in order to atone
for their base deed
they had to complete
a series of tasks.
The final task was to
give three shouts
from the top of the
Hill of Miodhchaoin.
This task was not,
however, as it easy
as it seemed: King
Miodhchaoin's sons
were friends of the
murdered Cian, and
the king refused to
allow the brothers
to climb the hill to
shout. This refusal
led to a battle in
which the Tureinn
brothers killed the
sons of Miodhchaoin,
but not without
themselves receiving
mortal wounds.

and thus be free of obligation. There now remained only two tasks: to acquire the cooking spit and to give three shouts from the hill of King Miodhchaoin. To gain the spit, Brian made a magical suit out of water lilies, descended into the sea between Ireland and Britain to find the island of Fianchuive, and so charmed the 150 maidens who guarded the spit that they gave up their virginity as well as the spit. That completed, the three went to the Hill of Miodhchaoin to give their three shouts. But King Miodhchaoin's three sons had been friends of the murdered Cian, and the king refused to give the sons of Tureinn permission to ascend the hill. A fierce battle ensued that ranged the length of Ireland before the villainous brothers triumphed. Despite being badly wounded, the brothers crawled to the top of the hill and gave the requisite three shouts, then immediately returned to Magh Tuiredh to report their success to Lugh and to be healed by the magic pigskin that they had already given him. Remembering the brutal murder of his father, Lugh refused their request and the three died in great agony to the immense pleasure of the young king.

THE COMING OF THE GAELS: THE LAST MYTHOLOGICAL INVASION OF IRELAND

The sons of Tureinn steal the magical chariot and horses of King Dobar of Sicily. Note that one brother drives the chariot in the time-honored Celtic way, by standing on the trace.

The victorious Tuathans enjoyed their good fortune for only a few years. On May 1—again the sources neglect the year—a new and strange race landed on the southern coast of Ireland at a place called Ihbhear Sceine. These people were known as the Sons of Mil or, more simply, the Gaels. Supposedly, they came from Spain, which at that time was called Iberia. Some linguists believe that the name Mil is a rendition of the Latin word *miles*, which means "soldiers," and that these soldiers also named their new home Iberia, which gradually evolved into Hibernia—the name by which Ireland was known in the ancient and medieval worlds. Whatever the evolution of Ireland's name, this mythical

This terra-cotta head, which is now in the Museo Civico, Bologna, Italy, was originally part of a temple frieze in Bassoferato, Italy.

Gaels realized they had been tricked, and Amhairghin invoked still more powerful magic; the contrary wind died, and the invaders once more stormed ashore, angry at this treachery. The Battle of Tailtiu followed, and the warriors and magic of the Tuatha proved no match for the Sons of Mil. The two sides agreed to a treaty, but the Tuatha proved untrustworthy, harassing the Gaels by stunting their crops of wheat and reducing the flow of milk from their cows.

Under duress, the Tuatha accepted a new treaty by which they withdrew underground to live in the *sidhs*, the Neolithic burial mounds that can be found throughout Ireland. There the Tuatha de Danu lived a wonderful life in perfect harmony with one another. The sidhs were said to have their own sky, green grass, trees, and brooks. Inside them was constant feasting, song, and sport, as well as an endless supply of beautiful women. The residents were ageless and free from disease. Each sidh had its own magic cauldron that produced an inexhaustible supply of food, and the inhabitants spent their time feasting, making love, and fighting (the fighting produced no permanent wounds). It is to the sidhs that the dead traveled to join in this eternal happiness. The living could also cross over into this sidh world and enjoy both the women and the food. While there, they stopped aging, but when they returned aboveground, to the real world, they immediately reverted to their true age, adding on the time they spent in the sidh. This happened to Oisin, the son of the Irish hero Finn mac Cumhail, who was lured into a sidh to be the lover of the beautiful Niamh. Oisin stayed with Niamh in her father's sidh for years, but eventually began yearning to return to the world above. Niamh warned him that he should not set foot on the earth and gave him a horse to ride out of the sidh. When Oisin returned to the world of mortals, he realized, to

account is no doubt the pale reflection of the historic arrival of some Celtic group in Ireland from the European continent.

The invaders were under the leadership of the warrior-poet-magician Amhairghin, who led his troops to the gates of Tara and there demanded the submission of the Tuatha de Danu. The Tuatha played for time, asking the Gaels to withdraw to the sea, or as they put it, "past the ninth wave from the shore." The ninth wave off shore was a magical barrier, and once the Gaels had passed beyond it, the Tuatha were certain their magic could raise a great wind that would prevent the attackers' return. But once beyond the ninth wave, the his surprise, that he had been away for three hundred years and immediately turned his horse around to reenter the sidh. Unfortunately, at that moment he fell off his horse, aging three hundred years the minute he touched the ground. He died a disfigured, wrinkled, and bent old man with whom the eternally lovely Niamh wanted nothing to do.

The Tuatha in their sidhs were ruled by the Daghdha, a hero god who waged war with the last Formorians. He carried a huge club, one end of which killed while the other healed any wound. The Daghdha was said to wander in and out of the sidhs, apparently immune to the aging process, wearing a tunic that was too short to cover his bottom. He was an odd combination of hero and buffoon with a huge sexual and gastronomic appetite. For instance, he was once captured by the Formorians and forced to eat a huge porridge made of eighty gallons (304L) of meal, eighty gallons of fat, and equal amounts of milk and wine, to which had been added eighty goats and eighty sheep. He attacked this mass of food with a spoon that needed four mortal men to lift it. When he had easily eaten it all, he seduced all the Formorian women, including the dread war goddess Morrighan, who, in gratitude for his attention, promised from then on to use her magic against her own people.

By and large, the Tuatha and the Gaels got along well after the establishment of the second truce, although the Tuatha occasionally returned to their old mischievous habit of stunting the Gaels' crops. There were numerous occasions of intermarriage between Gael men and Tuathan women, but comparatively few marriages between Gael women and Tuathan men.

Gael men were wise to treat the beautiful sidh women with great care and respect, for they possessed powerful magic. Once, for instance, Crunniuc mac Agnoman, a prince of Ulster, fell in love with a Tuathan beauty named Macha, daughter of Sainrith. She agreed to marry Crunniuc, but only if he swore never to tell anyone that she was the fleetest creature in the world. He promised, they married, and she soon became pregnant. From the size and shape of her belly it was clear that she would bear twins. Soon after, Crunniuc decided to take Macha to the fair, to show off her great beauty and to advertise his virility (as shown by her obvious pregnancy). At the fair they watched a chariot race in which the chariot of the king of Ulster took first place. Everyone said that the king's chariot was the fastest in the world, but Crunniuc, by this time full of beer, declared that he knew of someone faster. He immediately realized his slip and tried to cover it up, but upon close questioning by the king was forced to admit that the someone

When the Gaels invaded Ireland they drove the Tuatha de Danu underground, into the *sidhs* (the burial mounds that dot the Irish landscape). The sidhs were underground paradises, similar to the mortal landscape but more beautiful. Here the Tuatha indulged in endless feasting, drinking, and fighting, experiencing no pain or unhappiness and remaining forever young. Each year on the night of November 1, the Tuatha are said to leave their sidhs and move freely among mortals.

A human-headed horse from the lid of a pitcher found in a tomb near Reinheim, Germany. The human face on the horse is a classic example of Celtic art. The eyes and mouth are exaggerated characterizations of reality, and both the beard and the ears are pointed. This figure, which is now in a museum in Saarbrucken, Germany, dates from the fifth century B.C.

was his wife. The king was offended by the idea that a mere woman could outrun his magnificent horses, and threatened to put Crunniuc to death if his boast was not true.

Crunniuc went to Macha and begged her to run. She replied that she was unable to do so because she had already gone into labor. Crunniuc returned to the king with this news, but the king's honor was wounded and he ordered Macha brought before him. She came

as a dutiful subject, but pleaded not to be made to run in her condition. The king renewed his demand, and Macha agreed to run to save her boastful husband's life. She swore, however, that henceforth every man of Ulster, at some time during his early manhood years, would suffer pangs of childbirth equal to her own, and would need four months lying a-bed to recover. In the race Macha easily out-distanced the King's chariot, even in her ungainly condition. But the exertion aggravated her labor and once the race was over, Macha lay down on the fairgrounds and after a labor of five days and four nights gave birth to a baby boy and girl. During her hard labor and long convalescence Macha could barely move. True to her curse, every Ulsterman from then on suffered five days and four nights of racking pain from which he would require four months to recover. The place where Macha gave birth was named Emhain Macha, or the Twins of Macha, and the curse of Macha would return to haunt the men of Ulster in the hour of their greatest peril.

THE GREATEST IRISH MYTH: THE TAIN BO CUAILNGE

The set piece of all Irish mythology is the Tain Bo Cuailnge—the Cattle Raid of Cooley. It is the national epic of Ireland, akin to *The Iliad* for Greece, *Beowulf* for England, *El Cid* for Spain, and *The Song of Roland* for France. Furthermore, the Tain recounts, however dimly, an actual historical event that occurred sometime between 100 B.C. and A.D. 100. Cuchulainn, the hero of this story, probably was a real person, as were most of the other characters in the myth. A number of other characters, such as the wicked Queen Maeve of Connacht and Lugh mac Ethnenn, were originally Celtic deities that Christian copyists metamorphosed into earthly beings—albeit ones with great magical powers.

The myth survived the ages in three ancient Irish manuscripts: the *Book of the Dun Cow*, the *Yellow Book of Lecan*, and the *Book of Leinster*. The oldest of these, the *Book of the Dun Cow*, was written by the monk Maelmuiri

before 1106, but it is certainly a copy of an earlier eighth-century rendition. In places, however, the language is the Irish Gaelic spoken centuries before that.

The language in the *Book of the Dun Cow* is so earthy and blunt that Lady Gregory, a fine translator but a proper Victorian woman, who first translated the Tain into English, left out much that she felt was improper and lewd. Queen Maeve, for instance, needed nine men in a row to satisfy her lust (a fact Lady Gregory certainly omitted), and was therefore known as Maeve the friendly thighed. Queen Maeve was classically evil and also a great sorceress who could change her shape to accomplish her ends. She murdered with abandon, browbeat her long-suffering husband, King Ailill, whose death she finally arranged, and was killed by her nephew Furbraidhe (she had killed his mother, who was her sister), using his sling and a piece of hard cheese instead of a stone. Maeve is so evil and lustful that it is hard not to feel that her character may have been exaggerated by a celibate and no doubt repressed Christian monk anxious to prove the evil nature of women.

The language of the Tain is also grisly in its descriptions of battles. Brains are constantly being dashed out, leaking out of ears and eyes, or splashing over nearby people. Heads are cut off, split in half, or crushed to pulp, while hands, arms, legs, and testicles are lopped off with abandon. Wounded warriors trip over their own intestines, which descend from holes in their stomachs cut by sweeping attacks with sword or spear. In these descriptions, the Tain easily exceeds similar discussions of battles in the heroic literature of other peoples; certainly *The Iliad*, long touted as the great bloodfest of Western literature, cannot equal the Tain for bloody detail.

The Tain Bo Cuailnge begins with a bedtime chat between Queen Maeve and her husband, King Ailill of Connacht. During this

The famous bedroom
argument between
King Ailill and Queen
Maeve that led to the
great cattle raid
of Cuailnge (the Tain
Bo Cuailnge).

conversation, Maeve demanded a comparison of her possessions with those of her husband. This simple discussion quickly expanded into a full accounting that consumed the whole night as scribes and accountants, hurriedly summoned from bed, brought in lists enumerating the jewelry, swords, lands, cattle, sheep, pigs, and stallions of both Maeve and Ailill. Maeve became angered when she found that for each item of value she had, Ailill had one of equal value. At this point, it seemed to be a tie, but Ailill, now caught up in the competition, had one card yet to play—he threw into the accounting his great white horned bull, Finnbennach, who copulated daily with fifty heifers, leaving them all with calves. Maeve had nothing to match this—a fact that especially galled her since Finnbennach had originally been one of her bulls, but had left and become the top bull of Ailill's herds because he would not be owned by a woman.

Beaten in the accounting, Maeve decided that she needed a bull to match her husband's. She soon learned from her chamberlain, Mac Roth, that the only bull that could match Finnbennach was Donn Cuailnge, the great brown bull belonging to Daire mac Fiachna, who lived in Ulster under King Conchobar mac Nessa. Maeve immediately dispatched Mac Roth to Daire mac Fiachna to ask the loan of the bull for a year so that she

might raise a whole herd of bulls more than equal to Ailill's Finnbennach. For this loan she offered Daire fifty heifers, land, a war chariot worth twenty-one female slaves, and her own "friendly thighs." If he could not negotiate for the bull, Maeve told Mac Roth, then he should steal it. Mac Roth succeeded in getting Daire to agree to loan the bull, but the night before Mac Roth was to return to Connacht with the bull, one of Daire's servants overheard Mac Roth's retainers talking about the alternative plan to steal the bull had negotiations broken down. When the servants told Daire this news, he became angry, feeling he had been insulted, and sent Mac Roth home empty-handed.

When Mac Roth returned without the prize, Maeve bullied Ailill into amassing an army to invade Ulster and steal the bull. The army that Maeve and Ailill gathered was huge and filled with famous fighters. There were three thousand men from Leinster as well as three thousand exiles from Ulster who, for one reason or another, had fled the rule of King Conchobar. Even Conchobar's son, Cormac, was a member of this army of exiles. In addition to these forces, there was the main Connacht army, and thanks to the persuasive Maeve, soon all of Ireland had joined in this venture to obtain the great bull of Cuailnge. Yet even before the fighting started, Maeve had signs that her unholy quest would fail. Her husband counseled caution and tried to turn aside his wife's desire for the bull. The prophetess Fedelm, he said, had seen the future: the Connacht army red with blood. Even the best warrior in the army, Ferghus mac Roich, predicted disaster.

As Maeve was considering all these predictions of doom and gloom, word reached her that the entire army of Ulster had been incapacitated by the curse of Macha uttered many years before. The Ulster men were seized with labor pains and would be in agony for days and convalescing for four months thereafter. In all of Ulster only one man, a boy really, was untouched by the curse—Cuchulainn, who was only seventeen years old, too young to suffer the curse of Macha. Maeve laughed aside the warning of Fedelm that the boy would ruin her army and ordered the invasion of Ulster to begin.

The stage is thus set for the heroic story of one boy—albeit an exceptional boy—who stood alone against impossible odds in defense of his country. It is an image that continues to inspire the Irish today. There is, for instance, a heroic bronze statue of Cuchulainn in the lobby of the General Post Office in Dublin. The comparison has not been lost on the Irish during their struggle for independence from the British Empire, with the

The relief of a bull in the bottom of the Gundestrup Cauldron (see page 21). Bulls were especially valued by the Celts, and it is not surprising that two Celtic nations might go to war over one of these prized animals.

OPPOSITE: These four heads, which were found at the second century B.C. oppidum at Entremont, France, may be carvings of actual heads taken in battle. It was common for Celtic warriors to adorn their homes and temples with the severed heads of their enemies. These are now in the Musée Granet, Aix-en-Provence, France.

BELOW RIGHT: Stone pillars inscribed with ogham characters. In his ongoing battles during the Tain Bo Cuailnge, Cuchulainn wrote challenges to his Connacht enemies in ogham. The word *ogham* is taken from the name Ogmios, the Celtic god of eloquent speech. About 375 examples of the ogham alphabet survive in Ireland. Originally, the ogham alphabet contained twenty characters composed of combinations of straight lines and notches cut along an incised vertical line or along the vertical edge of an upright stone or wooden pillar. The Celts derived the idea for their alphabet from the Romans; they did not use the Latin letters because most of these had curved designs, which were difficult to carve into stone or wood.

British representing the huge forces of Queen Maeve, and the Irish Republican Army (IRA) as the modern descendant of Cuchulainn standing against the horde.

The Connacht army moved east and Maeve soon showed her evil, unbalanced nature. One evening she saw that the Leinster contingent of her army had set up camp more quickly than the men of her own country. Jealous of their performance, Maeve contemplated sending them home, but then decided, arbitrarily, that it would be better to kill them. Her husband was shocked and pointed out the negative effect that this action would have on the troops, recommending that the Leinster group instead be broken up and the men distributed throughout the rest of the army. Maeve reluctantly agreed.

Shortly after this, the Connacht men had their first encounter with Cuchulainn at a ford, and this encounter was a harbinger of the problems this boy would cause. Scouts found a wooden horse hobble on which ogham characters had been carved. The carved characters spelled out a challenge stating that no one could cross the ford unless there existed in the army of Maeve and Ailill a man who could carve such a hobble with one

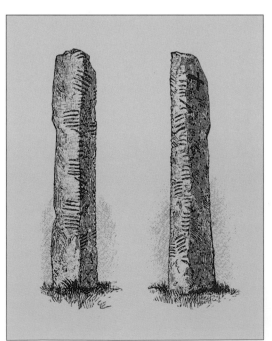

hand. (Apparently, Cuchulainn's hands were so large that he was able to perform this trick.) Since no one could do this (try carving anything with one hand!), the army, under the rather formalized rules of warfare that seem completely out of step in today's brutal world, was forced to find another ford to cross.

At the next ford Cuchulainn killed four scouts and cut off their heads; with a single stroke he sliced off a tree branch as thick as a man's thigh, then mounted the heads on the stick, placing this grisly trophy in the middle of the ford. Cuchulainn covered the branch with ogham characters stating that no Connacht man could cross at that ford unless there was a man in the army who could cut a similar tree branch with one sword stroke. The Connacht army once more turned aside, for they could not meet this challenge. As they marched down the road, they again found the way blocked, this time by a huge downed oak bearing an ogham inscription forbidding use of the road unless the Connacht men had someone who could jump the oak in his chariot. While the attention of the army was fixed on this obstacle, Cuchulainn sneaked up and killed Orlam, the son of Maeve and Ailill, in a duel.

The goal of Cuchulainn was to slow down the invaders until the Ulstermen could recover from their illness. He adopted terror tactics, slaughtering soldiers at long range with his sling and even shooting Maeve's pet squirrel off her neck and Ailill's pet bird off his head. Cuchulainn took to aiming stones at Maeve with such unerring accuracy that she was unable to appear anywhere in camp save with a bodyguard of shield men surrounding her on all four sides. By now the army was completely terrified and many men demanded an explanation of who this incredible boy was. Only one man, Ferghus mac Roich, could tell them. Ferghus was a friend of Cuchulainn and an exile from Ulster. His

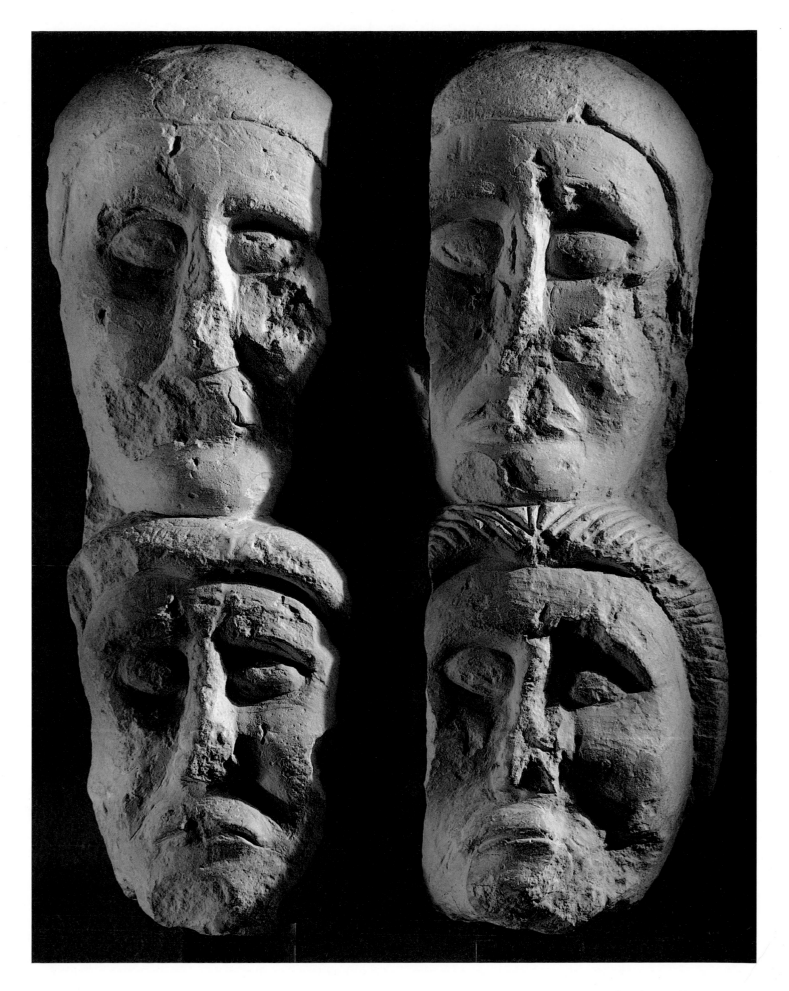

These small statues—
one of an elk, the
other of a wild boar—
date from the second
century B.C. They
are now in the
Landesmuseum,
Veduz, Liechtenstein.
The holes in the body
of the elk probably
held semiprecious
stones.

friendship with Cuchulainn prevented his fighting the young man (another of the customs of war at that time), even though the Tain leaves no doubt that he could have done so with a reasonable chance of success. Ferghus was a giant with the strength of seven hundred men and could eat seven deer, seven boars, and seven cows, all washed down with seven tubs of beer, at one sitting.

Ferghus explained that Cuchulainn was the son of Lugh mac Ethnenn, the hero who had led the Tuatha de Danu to victory over the Formorians; he was also the son of Sualdam the Smith. (In Irish mythology there is no impediment to a hero having two fathers, one divine and one human; this merely adds to his strength.) His mother was Deichtine, the sister of King Conchobar of Ulster. At the age of seven the young Cuchulainn, who at that time bore the name Setanta, left home to seek his fortune at the court of King Conchobar. During his journey to the court, the boy entertained himself by hitting his ball with his bat, then throwing the bat after the ball so that it hit the ball while it was in the air, driving it farther, and then hurled his spear so

that it struck the bat, pushing it after the ball. He then sprinted ahead to catch the ball, the bat, and the spear before they hit the ground, repeating the process all the way to the royal residence at Emhain Macha.

When Setanta reached the vicinity of the palace, he saw 150 boys—the sons of the noblest warriors of Ulster—practicing for war. Since he was a stranger, they decided to rough him up a little, and they threw their spears at him. To their surprise he caught or deflected every one of the spears with his shield, and when they threw their clubs at him he dodged them. By this time the youngster was angry, and he rushed the group, beating fifty of them so badly that it took them three years to recover. The rest of the boys ran to the safety of the king. Standing boldly before King Conchobar, Setanta identified himself as the king's nephew, and the king invited him to join the boy troop and become its leader.

Later, Setanta was attacked by a huge dog that belonged to the blacksmith Culann, and had to kill the dog in self-defense. When Culann complained that he now had no one to guard his forge and tools, Setanta volunteered to stand in place of the dog: "I will be your hound and guard your forge until another dog can be trained." In gratitude, Culann renamed the boy Cuchulainn, which means "hound of Culann."

Soon after this, he single-handedly killed the three sons of the outlaw Fer Ulli and rode back to Emhain Macha with their heads dangling from his saddle. During this fight, he had been seized with a berserker rage in which he changed physically, growing in stature while his hair stood on end. His right eye shrank to the size of a pin and his left eye grew to the size of a saucer, his lips turned back in a deathly grin, and his body temperature increased to such a level that his mere presence ignited nearby trees and dwellings. In this altered state he was unable to tell friend from foe and sought to kill everyone within reach. His charioteer ran back to Emhain Macha, where he told the king of Cuchulainn's changes. Conchobar, apparently experienced in these matters, sent all the women in court out to meet the returning hero with their breasts exposed—this apparently was the time-honored way to deal with a hero's berserk frenzy. Still, it required three baths in ice-cold water to return the boy's temperature to normal.

When Ferghus had finished his tale of Cuchulainn, it required all the forcefulness of Maeve's personality, plus aspersions cast on their manliness, to get the army to remain in the field. In the succeeding days, Cuchulainn challenged various individuals to single combat. Either by magic, cajoling, or the promise of sexual favors, Maeve was able to find individual champions to fight Cuchulainn almost daily. When all these challengers failed, Maeve sent men to attack him at night, even though this was a serious breach of etiquette. It made no difference, however, for Cuchulainn met this treachery and effortlessly defeated all comers. When the hero Nad-

cranntail came against him with nine spears of holly, the youngster deflected each spear easily and without ceasing his activity of trying to catch birds. Later, when Cuchulainn was practicing his trick of walking along the length of a spear in flight, the warrior Cur mac Calath attacked him with a spear and Cuchulainn threw an apple core he was eating at the man, splitting Cur's head open. Only once did he come close to defeat, when Gail Dana and his twenty-eight sons attacked him all at once, using poisoned weapons. This was so unfair that one of Maeve's own soldiers, an exiled Ulsterman named Fiachna mac Fir Febe, came to the aid of Cuchulainn, helping him to kill all twenty-nine attackers.

Finally, despite repeated successes, after almost a month of daily single combat punctuated by pauses only long enough for the

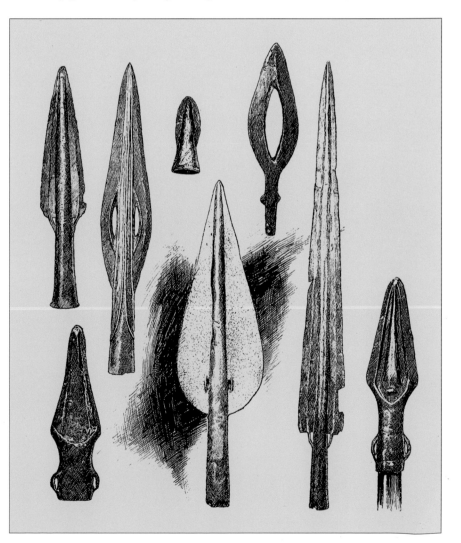

This collection of Irish spearheads, all of which were found in Irish rivers, may have topped some of the spears thrown at Cuchulainn by the 150 sons of the noblest warriors of Ulster.

Connacht men to clear their own dead away so that fresh attackers could attack, Cuchulainn began to tire. He had not slept all this time and had caught only a little rest by standing up leaning on his spear. In Cuchulainn's time of need, however, his father, Lugh mac Ethnenn, came back from the land of the dead to take up the challenges and allow his son to get three days of sleep. While his son slept, Lugh treated his wounds so that the young hero awakened refreshed and ready for battle. Lugh also left his son a chariot and horse, both armored with spikes, plus special body armor made of twenty-seven layers of cowhide. Thus equipped and rested, Cuchulainn went on the offensive, taking the battle to the enemy. He underwent the berserker rage and physical changes that had first happened in his youth, and in a single attack killed five hundred nobles, including 130 kings, and an unspecified number of commoners. In a towering rage, he slaughtered women and children, too. By the time Cuchulainn's berserker rage had passed, the bodies were piled up six deep. This rampage came to be called Seisrech Bresligi, the Sixfold Slaughter.

At last the wicked Maeve found a champion to match Cuchulainn—his own foster brother, Ferdia mac Damain. Ferdia had stayed away from the fight out of respect for his brother, but Maeve used a combination of ridicule and the promise of marriage to her beautiful daughter Finnebair to persuade Ferdia to take up the challenge. The duel was titanic and lasted four days. Each day, the two fought with different weapons: on the first day, darts and shields with razor-sharp rims; on the second, spears and shields; and on the

third, short stabbing spears. At the close of each day, the warriors rested, making camp together and treating one another's wounds. Finally, on the fourth day, Ferdia allowed Cuchulainn the choice of weapons; the hero chose to fight with his own personal weapon, the *gae bolga*, a spear with five points, each of which would spring open into a clump of seven barbs once it entered the body, making it impossible to pull out except by cutting away huge clumps of flesh. The gae bolga was always launched with Cuchulainn's right foot, and was known to never miss its mark. The valiant Ferdia was wounded, and died with Cuchulainn expounding on his dead brother's courage and skill with arms.

Following this four-day battle, the Ulstermen recovered from their ailment and began to march to support Cuchulainn. They were goaded into action by Cuchulainn's mortal father, Sualdam, who had gone to Emhain Macha to plead with King Conchobar for aid. Unfortunately, while delivering his plea,

The Tain Bo Cuailnge climaxes with an incredible battle between the two great bulls—the white bull Finnbennach and the brown bull Donn Cuailnge. The battle rages across the plain of Muirhevra, with Donn Cuailnge emerging victorious (though he later succumbs to mortal wounds incurred during the battle) and Finnbennach's body parts and internal organs scattered across the landscape.

Sualdam had tripped, fallen against the razor-sharp edge of a shield, and cut off his own head. To the amazement of everyone, the severed head had continued its appeal on Cuchulainn's behalf, pleading that the Ulstermen, even if not completely recovered, needed to begin marching to Cuchulainn's aid. Twenty great companies marched; so great were their numbers that the breath of so many men was confused for morning fog.

The final battle between Cuchulainn and the Ulstermen, on one side, and the forces of Queen Maeve and King Ailill, on the other, was one gigantic melee in which the war chariots and infantry were packed so tightly together as they fought that one could drive a chariot over them from one end of the battlefield to the other without touching the ground. The exiled Ulsterman Ferghus mac Roich, who had been with the Connacht army throughout, now joined the battle but sought to avoid a confrontation with his friend Cuchulainn. At one point Ferghus came close to killing King Conchobar of Ulster, but Conall Cernach restrained him in midstroke by telling him that killing the king would earn him too many enemies. "But how

then will I vent my anger?" cried Ferghus. Conall Cernach suggested that he use his strength to slash off the tops of three nearby mountains. Ferghus did so in three mighty hacks and felt much relieved.

In this last great melee, even Maeve waded into the battle, killing one hundred men with her spear before withdrawing from the field. In the last moments of the fight, Cuchulainn actually came face-to-face with Maeve and briefly toyed with the idea of killing her. He decided not to, exclaiming, "I do not kill women," apparently forgetting the women and children he had slain during the Sixfold Slaughter.

The last act of this great epic comes about when the objects of it all, the great bull Finnbennach and the brown bull Donn Cuailnge, meet to fight. The struggle between these mighty beasts lasted all night, and at dawn the Ulster army saw Donn Cuailnge wandering across the plain of Muirhevra with the bones and internal organs of Finnbennach hanging from his horns. The great bull, mortally wounded, staggered about looking for water with pieces of his beaten enemy dropping off his horns. To this day, the poet of the

Tain tells us, Ath Luain (Loin Ford) marks the place where the great testicles dropped off, Finn Lethe (Shoulder Blade River) the spot where Finnbennach's shoulder blade fell off, and Tromma (Liver) Spring the site where the great bull's liver came to rest. Finally, Donn Cuailnge lay down and died at Druim Tairb, or Bull Ridge.

There is a final irony in the ending that seems typically Irish. Heroes and armies struggled for a month, and thousands died over the silly whim of a wicked woman only to see the object of that whim—the great bull—die unclaimed by either side.

BRICRIU'S FEAST

While much of Irish mythology deals with war, as illustrated by the Tain Bo Cuailnge, a good portion of it has to do with Irish social life—although even there fighting and violence seem to have been the norm. One of the most famous of these tales has to do with Bricriu Nemthenga and the great feast he gave for the Irish heroes. This story is found in Maelmuiri's twelfth-century *Book of the Dun Cow*, but dates from at least five hundred years earlier. Something of Bricriu's personality is apparent from his cognomen, for Nemthenga means "Poison Tongue."

Bricriu Poison Tongue was a man who enjoyed controversy. He loved witnessing disputes and he enjoyed causing them even more, especially if they ended in bloodshed. One year he decided to work a great mischief that he hoped would bring the greatest heroes in Ireland into conflict with one another. He planned carefully. First, he built a huge feast hall at Tech Midchuarta that was grander in size than the royal palace of King Conchobar at Emhain Macha, and certainly more resplen-

dent with gold and silver overlay than any palace in the world. The dining room alone was a huge chamber surrounded with thirty elaborate pillars so tall that seven men and a team of oxen were required to place each one, and thirty Druids were needed to plan each placement. The hall included private apartments for each guest, but the most fascinating room in the the place was a secret chamber from which Bricriu Poison Tongue could watch the goings-on in the dining room and not be seen—he planned to use this room to observe with delight the disputes he would engineer among his guests.

When at the end of a year the hall was finished, Bricriu traveled to Emhain Macha to

This stone head, which dates from the second century B.C. and was found at the Celtic sanctuary of Msecke Zehrovice near Prague, Czech Republic, is another classic example of Celtic art.

OPPOSITE: In the climactic scene from Bricriu's Feast, in which the mischief maker Bricriu instigates a rivalry among the heroes Loeguire Buadach, Conall Cernach, and Cuchulainn over who should receive the champion's portion, the feasting hall of Bricriu is stormed by the wives of these heroes, accompanied by their 150 attendants. As Cuchulainn lifts the corner of the hall (bottom left) to let his wife in, Bricriu and his wife fall out of the second-story window and into a garbage pit.

invite King Conchobar and the heroes to a feast. He described the preparations and the food, told the nobles of the accommodations they would enjoy, and promised not to bring about any discord. But Ferghus mac Roich did not believe him, and he warned the nobles that no good would come of attending this feast for, he said, "Bricriu cannot help but be himself and longs to set warrior against warrior, servant against servant, and wife against wife." At this, Bricriu became angry and swore that while he would promise not to use his poison tongue at the feast he would certainly use it if the court did not attend! He threatened that he would use his evil gift of lies and deceit to set father against son, brother against brother, and mother against daughter. He further claimed that he possessed a magic incantation that would set the right breast of every woman in Ulster rubbing against the left one until both were so badly chapped and sore that every woman in the kingdom would be miserable and would make her husband miserable, too. Faced with these threats, the Ulster nobility agreed to come, but they demanded certain guarantees: Bricriu would have to provide hostages to guarantee his good behavior and was forbidden to attend the feast itself, the assumption being that if Bricriu knew he could not observe dissension he would not want to cause any. None of the nobles, however, knew of the secret chamber Bricriu had built above the dining room.

Hardly had Bricriu extracted the nobles' promises to attend before he started to sow trouble. He approached each of the three greatest warriors—Loeguire Buadach, Conall Cernach, and Cuchulainn—separately and said, "You are the greatest warrior in Ireland and so you deserve the champion's portion at the feast." He described what the champion's portion would be, and it was truly amazing. A seven-year-old boar that had eaten nothing but oatmeal, milk, nuts, and wheat all its life

had been stewed in a cauldron big enough for three men to sit in, along with a seven-year-old cow that had been fed the same diet as the boar. This meaty broth had been simmered with wine until the meat was fit for the gods. Each hero, thinking he alone had been asked by the host to take the champion's portion, agreed to claim it when the servants brought it in. Bricriu hoped to watch the resultant battle from the safety of his hidden room. He was not disappointed.

Within minutes of being seated, all three heroes had claimed the champion's portion, and had fallen to blows to enforce their claim. Their brightly polished swords clashed so swiftly that witnesses claimed it looked as though lightning were in the house. Conall Cernach and Loeguire Buadach quickly turned their attention to Cuchulainn, and the unfairness of two on one caused King Conchobar and Ferghus mac Roich to intervene and separate the three. The king declared that no one would get the champion's portion that night, but all would share equally. The next night, according to the king, they would all make a judgment as to who would receive the next champion's portion.

Now, however, Bricriu saw a further opportunity to cause trouble. He left his room and went secretly to the wives of each of the three heroes, who were preparing to enter the hall to sit with their husbands. First to Fedelm, Loeguire's wife, then to Lendalair, Conall's wife, and finally to Emer, Cuchulainn's wife, Bricriu made the following statement: "You are clearly more beautiful than the wives of your husband's rivals and your spouse is clearly the best of the three, therefore you and your retinue should by right enter the feast hall first. In fact, I insist on it!" Impressed with Bricriu's statement, the three women, each with fifty attendants, began marching toward the hall, all determined to get there first. At first, the three groups moved

As the argument over who will get the champion's portion continues, the heroes undergo a series of tests. In attempting to complete the first test, Loeguire Buadach and Conall Cernach are defeated by a giant who steals their swords, armor, and chariots. Cuchulainn later confronts and defeats this giant in the misty forest, and retrieves his rivals' possessions.

with stately pomp, but when they caught sight of one another, they gradually increased their speed to arrive first at the door. Within moments, 153 women were running hell-bent for the door with their skirts hitched up well past the point of modesty. Inside, the warriors felt the tremor of this advancing horde and, fearing an attack by enemies, ordered the door shut. The women reached the door and began yelling for admission. Each man, hearing his wife's voice, strove to force open the door, but King Conchobar, disgusted with the lack of dignity, forbade it. Nevertheless, Loeguire and Conall smashed holes in the walls of the hall and pulled their women inside. Cuchulainn merely bent down, worked his hand under the wall of the feast

hall, and raised one side of the hall high enough so his wife could come inside. Needless to say, the rest of the women streamed in through the opening, and complete chaos reigned at the feast.

By now, Bricriu should have been helpless with laughter, but Cuchulainn's stunt had toppled Bricriu and his wife out a window and down into the garbage pit outside the hall. Covered with muck, Bricriu ran to the door and demanded admission to his own hall. At first the gatekeeper did not recognize him because of his foul covering, but Bricriu pushed past and angrily claimed the feast was over unless he who had tilted the hall set it right. Cuchulainn grasped the tilted wall and easily set the hall straight again. Nevertheless, for that night the feasting was ruined, and everyone retired.

The next morning King Conchobar suggested that each warrior prove his right to the champion's portion by performing a great deed; the three heroes—Loeguire, Conall, and Cuchulainn—immediately set out to find suitable adventures. Loeguire went first, but was stopped by a mist and a giant with a club who stole his chariot and sword and then ran him off. Next, Conall came along, found the same mist, and was also deprived of chariot and sword by the giant. Last was Cuchulainn, who also met the mist and the giant. He not only killed the giant, but brought back the possessions of both Loeguire and Conall. The assembled nobles wanted to declare him the winner of the champion's portion for that night, but Loeguire and Conall whined that the mist and the giant were tricks of the people of the sidh, who were known to be friends of Cuchulainn. King Conchobar, who wished to be completely fair, refused Cuchulainn the victory and declared that there would be no award of a champion's portion for that night.

In the morning the three men once again set out. This time they traveled to Connacht

to let King Ailill and Queen Maeve decide who would receive the portion. Although there is never a clear chronology in Irish mythology, this event must have taken place before the Tain Bo Cuailnge because Ailill and Maeve appeared happy to see Cuchulainn and soon decided that he deserved the champion's portion. The young hero had defeated a giant cat that tried to steal his meal, hurled a chariot wheel through the palace roof, and tossed one hundred needles into the air one at a time in such a way that each needle went through the eye of the needle just thrown. When all the needles had been thrown, they fell to earth in an interconnected chain. As if that was not enough, Cuchulainn cleared the palace of the ghosts who had sent Loeguire and Conall running in fright. After performing these deeds, Cuchulainn was quickly deemed the most worthy.

However, Maeve and Ailill did not publicly declare their choice. Instead, they called each hero to them separately, gave each a cup, and declared him the winner secretly. Loeguire got a bronze cup, Conall a silver cup, and Cuchulainn a cup of red gold. Apparently, Maeve and Ailill did not want to declare a winner for fear the losers would wreck the palace. To prevent this, they obtained a promise from each to return to Bricriu's feast hall before he showed his victory trophy. Once the three returned, Cuchulainn's cup made it obvious to all that he was the winner, but Loeguire and Conall again planted a seed of doubt in King Conchobar's mind by swearing that Cuchulainn had bought the cup instead of earning it. Once again the champion's portion went unclaimed.

The next day the three contestants set off for the lake where the great Druid Uath son of Imoman lived. After the warriors told Uath why they had come, the Druid made all three promise to undergo a certain ordeal and to

abide by his decision as to who deserved the champion's portion. Uath declared that each hero would cut off the Druid's head and on the following day Uath would get to cut off the hero's head. Loeguire, who went first, accepted the challenge because he was certain that Uath could not live without his head. He sliced off Uath's head and was horrified to see the Druid stand, pick up his head, and walk off. The next morning, Uath was at the lake with his head firmly on his shoulders, but Loeguire was nowhere to be seen. It was now Conall's turn, and he, thinking that perhaps Loeguire had botched the job, struck off the Druid's head with a mighty whack. Again, the headless body stooped, picked up the head, and stalked off into the forest. The next morning, Conall was nowhere to be seen, but Uath was there waiting for Cuchulainn to cut off his head. Cuchulainn easily struck off the head and watched the Druid leave. The next morning, however, unlike his two cowardly predecessors, he duly laid his head on a tree stump and awaited Uath's blow. Uath took a

The Celtic fascination with decapitation is further exemplified by this 4-inch (10cm) silver plaque, which dates from the first century B.C. and is now in the Museo Romano, Brescia, Italy.

head of the sea giant, twenty-seven other heads, and the heart of the monster, which he had ripped from its body through the creature's throat. Faced with this indisputable evidence, Loeguire and Conall could not deny Cuchulainn's prowess, but they convinced King Conchobar that since the deeds were done outside Ulster, they could not apply to the naming of an Ulster champion.

By now Cuchulainn was disgusted with the whole sorry mess and withdrew from the contest. But fate took a hand, for as the king and his court sat at Emhain Macha, a truly hideous ogre shambled into the audience hall. His head was huge and had such a growth of tangled, dirty hair that thirty calves could have found shelter there from winter storms. His yellow eyes were the size of cauldrons, each finger was thicker than a man's wrist, and he carried an ax that twenty oxen could not pull. The ogre made the same challenge that Uath the Druid had made. When no one took up the challenge, the honor of Ulster fell under question, and the king ordered that Cuchulainn be summoned. Rather than see his country dishonored, Cuchulainn accepted the challenge. He sliced off the ogre's head and, just as he had suspected, watched the monster stoop, pick up the head, and leave the hall. The next morning, the creature was back, and true to his word, Cuchulainn put his head on the block to await the blow. The ogre made as if to cut off the head, but in the midst of the downward stroke reversed the ax and brought the flat end down onto the hero's neck. At that moment the ogre changed shape and became Uath, who was still angry that his decision had not been honored. The king, shamed by his poor judgment, declared that henceforth Cuchulainn would be acknowledged as the greatest warrior in all Ireland, and with that everyone returned to Bricriu's feast hall to watch the hero eat his champion's portion.

large ax and swung it high above his head as if to cut off the hero's head, but at the last moment he reversed the blade so that the flat side struck Cuchulainn's neck. Uath then declared Cuchulainn the winner and truly worthy of the champion's portion. To the amazement of many, Loeguire and Conall nevertheless protested the decision since, as they pointed out, no one had been there to witness the exchange between Uath and Cuchulainn, and without witnesses the decision was invalid. Again the champion's portion went unclaimed.

The next morning, the members of the court set out for the castle of Cu Rui mac Dare, where, without much trouble, Cuchulainn triumphed over a sea giant, twenty-seven attackers, and a fifty-foot (15m) monster. Loeguire and Conall, needless to say, ran at the first sign of danger. This time, however, Cuchulainn could prove his contention, for not only was the court there to witness, but he had the

THE FINN CYCLE—THE "OTHER" IRISH HERO

Cuchulainn is not the only Irish hero. Existing side by side with his legends are those of another hero, Finn mac Cumhail. To place Finn in his proper context, it is best to describe him as a mercenary captain of a band of roving soldiers, called a *fianna* in Irish Gaelic. Admission to this band of adventurers was difficult, for each *feinnidh*, or new recruit, had to pass two tests: He had to stand in a pit while every member of the Fianna threw a spear at him; if he flinched he was not acceptable. And he had to run through the forest with the whole fianna chasing after him; if they caught him he could not join the group. During this run the feinnidh could be disqualified if his hair caught on a branch or if a twig broke under his foot. Needless to say, everyone in the fianna was an exceptional warrior.

Finn himself was the most exceptional of the group. He had first shown his courage at the age of eight. At that time he had traveled to Tara just before the Feast of Samhain and noted the sad demeanor of the people. When he asked the meaning of this, an old Druid told him that every year at this time a giant wizard named Aillen mac Midna came to Tara and burned the place down. "Why don't the warriors just kill him?" asked the precocious eight-year-old. "Because Aillen mac Midna possesses a magic spell that causes everyone in Tara to fall asleep just before he comes, so there is no one awake to stop him," replied the old Druid. Finn laughed and said that he could easily kill this wizard. When the Druid reported the boy's comment to King Cormac mac Airt, he called Finn before him and asked how a mere child could hope to defeat such a powerful wizard. Finn would not divulge his plan, but he extracted a promise from the king that should he defeat the wizard he would become the most honored warrior in Tara. The king readily agreed.

On the day that the evil wizard was to arrive, Finn set his plan in motion. It was really quite simple—to prevent himself from falling asleep, he placed his sharp spear against his neck so that it would cut him slightly each time he began to doze off. Thus, when Aillen mac Midna cast his spell, the pain of the wound kept Finn awake even though everyone else in the city was in a deep sleep. As Aillen mac Midna prepared to burn down Tara, Finn got up and ran the giant through the back. It was not a particularly heroic attack, but it was courageous enough for an

A detail of the Witham Shield, which is now in the British Museum, London, England.

eight-year-old. The court was overjoyed to awaken the next day with a roof over their heads, and the king made Finn his champion.

As champion, Finn practiced constantly with weapons, but also set aside time to develop his intellect. He asked the court poet, Finnegas, to teach him poetry and other intellectual skills. One day as the two were fishing, Finn caught a huge fish that Finnegas recognized as the salmon of all knowledge. Finnegas and Finn cooked the salmon and ate it, thus gaining knowledge of all things. From then on, Finn was as liable to defeat an enemy through guile as by brute force.

Once, for instance, Finn used trickery to defeat a huge Scottish giant, in the process creating three famous geographical landmarks: the Giant's Causeway off the northern coast of Ireland near Rathlin Island, the Isle of Man in the Irish Sea, and Lough Neagh in the center of present-day Northern Ireland. Finn had heard from traveling bards that a Scottish giant was making fun of Finn's fighting ability and courage. Angered by this, Finn wrapped a challenge around a rock, took his sling, and cast the missile fifty miles (80km) across the Irish Sea to Scotland. The Scot got the message and also got "cold feet." He replied—by messenger, not by sling—that he would like to come to Ireland to take up the challenge but was unable to swim across the sea. Rather than give the giant an easy out, Finn pulled out his huge sword and hacked the great chunks of basalt that littered the coast of Ireland into five- and six-sided pillars. He then stuck these upright in the sea side by side so as to form a causeway from Scotland to Ireland. Now the giant had no excuse, and reluctantly he came across.

When the giant arrived at Finn's house, however, the Irish hero was nowhere to be seen. Finn's wife, the beautiful Sava, invited him in and said that Finn was away. She asked him to take a seat by the cradle. The giant sat

A portion of the Giant's Causeway, located off the northern coast of Ireland. The six-sided basalt columns are natural, but look so perfect and artificial that people have always suspected they were man-made. During World War II, a German U-boat commander, thinking that they were British coastal fortifications, went so far as to shell them.

down beside the cradle and the huge baby, who was over eighteen feet (5.5m) long, that was in it. The longer the giant sat there and looked at the huge baby, the more fearful he became, for, he reasoned, if this was Finn's baby—and Sava assured him it was—then how big must Finn be? As he sat pondering this, the baby reached out of the cradle and took the giant's hand. He stuck one of the giant's fingers into his mouth and bit it off! The baby chewed the finger well and swallowed it with a grin. That was too much for the giant, who jumped up, ran across the causeway, and never again made any comment about Finn's prowess as a fighter.

The baby, as it turned out, was really Finn in disguise. As soon as the giant left, Finn jumped up, ran to the coast, and began hurling huge clods of earth after him. The hole created by the removal of the largest clod, which Finn had torn up from the center of what is now Northern Ireland, filled with water and became Lough Neagh, the largest lake in Ireland. The chunk of earth fell into a shallow part of the Irish Sea, where it became the Isle of Man. To this day, geography teachers all over the world comment to their students on the similarity between the shape of Lough Neagh and that of the Isle of Man.

However, Finn was not always so clever. As he grew older, he began to have doubts about his physical prowess and, like so many aging men, decided to fortify and reassert himself with a young and beautiful wife. (Sava had died by this time.) He selected Grainne, the daughter of the High King of Ireland, and she—much against her will—accepted him because her father told her to. But she did not like him and resented her noblewoman's duty to marry for political considerations. Consequently, at her wedding feast she was bold with her glances, finally noting a handsome young man at the end of the table who was obviously of noble background. He was not only strong and virile, but had an intelligent mien, something that was lacking in many of the young warriors, who thought only of killing, drinking, and making love. She asked her nurse who he might be and the old woman scurried off to find out, returning soon after to announce that he was named Diarmaid ua Duibhne and that he was not only a fine warrior and poet but also had been blessed by the love god Oengus so that no woman could resist him. However, the old nurse went on to say that he was fickle, as befitted someone who could have his pick of women. This last bit of news made Grainne desire him all the more, and she decided to use him to escape her unhappy marriage as well as to satisfy her basic lust for him—for he was marvelously handsome in her eyes.

Grainne made a plan. With the help of her nurse she concocted a powerful sleeping

potion and secretly had the old woman slip it into the drinks of all the people at the banquet except Diarmaid. When everyone except Diarmaid fell asleep, Grainne approached and blatantly propositioned him. To her consternation he refused, saying that he was a member of Finn's fianna and could not dishonor his pledge to his lord. Grainne first tried to shame him by calling him a coward, but when this did not work she threatened him. "When everyone awakes tomorrow I will tell them you raped me, and who do you think they will believe? Who could doubt the truthfulness of a young bride?" Diarmaid, stuck for a solution, agreed to leave with her, still hoping he could find a way out of his predicament. The two fled into the forest.

The next morning, Finn awoke to find his bride missing. He finally shook the truth out of the old nurse, who had unaccountably

According to myth, the Isle of Man was formed when Finn mac Cumhail tore up a clod of earth to throw at a Scottish giant who had come to test Finn's fighting prowess. In another story, it is said that the Isle of Man was named for Manannan mac Lir, son of the Irish sea god Lir.

Toward the end of the Finn Cycle, Finn's beautiful young wife, Grainne, tricks the valiant hero Diarmaid, a member of Finn's *fianna* (his band of mercenaries), into sneaking off with her. Believing that Diarmaid has abducted his wife, Finn pursues them, and the two are aided by the Irish love god Oengus, who gives them an enchanted spear that grows in length when its wielder so chooses and a magical cloak that makes its wearer invisible. In this scene Finn and the other members of his fianna corner the lovers, but the two are able to escape as Diarmaid pole-vaults over the warriors and Grainne, wearing the cloak, sneaks quietly past her husband's troops.

stayed behind. Finn swore vengeance and pursued the couple with the whole fianna. The pursuit lasted seven years and ranged over all of Ireland and parts of Scotland. The first year, Diarmaid honorably resisted the sexual advances of Grainne, still hoping to find some way out of his dilemma and return her to her husband a virgin. He left signs at each of his campsites to show Finn that Grainne was still unsullied—a spotless white cloth, an uncarved haunch of venison, an unbroken loaf of bread, a jug of wine with the clay stopper intact. Still Finn pursued the two. At the end of the year, try as he might to avoid it, Diarmaid succumbed to her taunts. This pleased Oengus, the Irish love god, and he came to the aid of the two young fugitives. He gave them a magic cloak that conferred invisibility on whoever wore it, and a magic spear. Several times in the ensuing year these items saved the lovers. Once, when the two were trapped in a fortress, Diarmaid covered Grainne with the cloak and she easily slipped away unseen

through the very center of her husband's army. Diarmaid, meanwhile, used the spear, which could be magically lengthened, to pole-vault over the encircling enemy and thus make his escape.

After years of pursuit, Finn gave up, and the two lovers settled down, raised four children, and reached a reconciliation of sorts with Finn. Finn even allowed them to return to Tara, where the three lived in uneasy peace for a few years. But all the while, Finn, still worrying about his virility, plotted revenge. Finally he got his chance. One afternoon the fianna was out hunting and a huge boar gored Diarmaid, spilling his intestines out through a great hole in his belly. As he lay on the ground surrounded by the fianna, some of its members begged Finn to save Diarmaid. (Finn, it seems, had the magical ability to cure injuries by taking water in his hands—where it was magically changed into a healing balm—and then letting it flow over a wound.) Finn realized that he had his enemy in his power, but he also had the fianna looking on. He went to a nearby spring, took water in his cupped hands, and began to return to the wounded Diarmaid only to stumble purposely and let the water fall from his hands. He returned to the spring again to get more water, but once more stumbled and lost it. He then repeated this act once more. By this time, poor Diarmaid had lost too much blood, and while Finn was returning to the spring for a fourth try, the young man died. Everyone in the fianna suspected that Finn had allowed the young man to die, and this cast a shadow over the organization.

Grainne mourned for a year and then decided to make the best of things. To the disgust of all, she returned to Finn. Yet even in this seeming triumph, Finn was uneasy, for while he finally had Grainne, her past actions and flirtatious nature never allowed the old man a moment's peace. He was always imagining an affair between Grainne and a member of the fianna, or seeing meaningful and suspicious glances cast between his wife and some younger man. He became desperate to prove his strength and virility and tried to keep up with the youngest members of the fianna. One day during a jumping contest, he tried to leap the River Boyne, but fell in and drowned. Grainne remarried within the year.

The entrance to a sidh, or burial mound, in New Grange, County Lough, Ireland. This mound was built about 2500 B.C., long before the Celts arrived in Ireland. Each ruler of the Tuatha had his or her own sidh in which there was a tree that always bore fruit; a pig that, once slaughtered, was magically reborn the next day, so there was never a lack of meat; and a magic vat that always remained filled with beer.

THE
BRITISH MYTHS

The other collection of Celtic myths that has survived is from Wales. However, while there still exists a large number of Irish myths, all that survives from what must have been a large number of Welsh myths are the eleven stories found in a source called *The Mabinogion*.

Everything about *The Mabinogion* is vexing to scholars, even its title. The word *mabinogion* does not exist in Welsh—it is the result of the error made by the first English translator of the document, Lady Charlotte Guest, in the 1830s.

Although the Celtic legends of Britain predate the armor
worn by these knights by centuries, the Christian monks
who preserved the legends re-created the physical settings
of the myths in their own fourteenth-century world.

Snowdonia, Gwynedd, Wales. With its beautiful, mysterious landscape, Wales is the perfect setting for the Celtic tales preserved in *The Mabinogion*. The myth of Pwyll Lord of Dyfed and Rhiannon Daughter of Herveyd takes place in the vicinity of Harlech Castle, located on the northwestern coast of Wales.

She took the word *mabinogi* ("the early years"), mistranslated it as "the children's story," and added an *on* (which she thought was the correct plural ending) to make it "the children's stories." That was not the correct plural ending, but the name has stuck. And there is room for more confusion, for only the first four stories in the collection—Pwyll Lord of Dyfed, Branwen Daughter of Llyr, Manawydan Son of Llyr, and Math Son of Mathonwy are identified as mabinogi in the text. It would be most correct to title the collection *The Mabinogi and Other Myths*, but it is too late to do that after 160 years.

Equally vexing to scholars of Celtic mythology is the question of how long ago these myths were composed. The earliest copy of *The Mabinogion* that has survived is *The White Book of Rhydderch*, which was written about 1300, and that must have been many years after some bard first told the myths it contains. But there is no earlier source, or mention of an earlier source, to give a clue as to the myths' true age. Still, they must be ancient because they contain so many classic, early Celtic elements: the love of feasting and the emphasis on the otherworld (the sidh of Irish Celtic tales), to name only two. These early elements, however, sit beside much later medieval elements, such as chivalry, knights, ladies in distress, and jousting, all of which are products of continental literature that

developed long after the Celts. It is all very confusing, and many scholars have simply given up trying to sort it out.

Still, given what survives, scholars have been able to create a theory about how *The Mabinogion* came to combine Celtic and late medieval elements. Originally, the eleven myths in the collection traveled to France via Brittany, where they picked up some elements from the chivalric tradition before they once more crossed back over the English Channel to Wales. Hence these myths are different from the Celtic tales from Ireland, which never had the "advantage" of a continental experience. For instance, Irish myths are almost exclusively confined to Ireland, while the Welsh myths take place in Ireland, Wales, Scotland, France, and Italy. Irish myths describe combat in the classic Celtic style, with chariots, spears, and strange, fanciful weapons, but rarely armor. In the Welsh myths, there are armor, lances, jousting, tournaments, and warhorses, but never a mention of a chariot. Finally, the dialogue in the Irish Celtic myths is short and to the point, while that of the Welsh myths uses the flowery and polite conversation of the French nobility in the courtly love epics of the Continent.

One of the major literary elements of *The Mabinogion* that has long fascinated scholars is the book's preservation of the earliest attempt to portray King Arthur. This Arthur is far from the courtly king created by Chrétien de Troyes or William of Monmouth, yet he is certainly no crude Celtic chieftain; he is something in between.

Four of the most interesting myths in *The Mabinogion* are Lludd and Llevelys, Pwyll Lord of Dyfed and Rhiannon Daughter of Herveyd, Branwen Daughter of Llyr, and Gereint and Enid. If one can suggest a relative chronology for these four myths based on their content it would be as follows: Lludd and Llevelys is certainly the earliest, since it has the purest

Celtic elements and exhibits the least continental influence. The action is presented in a direct, no-nonsense fashion and includes a liberal sprinkling of magic and mythical monsters; it could be Irish. At the other extreme is Gereint and Enid, which is certainly the latest myth simply because it has the most chivalric atmosphere and clearly owes much to French literature. Pwyll Lord of Dyfed and Branwen Daughter of Llyr come somewhere in between. There is certainly Celtic magic and mystery in Pwyll's visit to the otherworld, and in the magical, regenerating cauldron that is part of Branwen's dowry, but there is also a good dose of courtliness and chivalry in these tales. Still, the best plan is not to overanalyze these stories, but simply to let them speak for themselves.

LLUDD AND LLEVELYS

Very early in the history of Britain there was a great king named Beli mac Mynogan who ruled wisely and well and had four sons: Lludd, Casswallawn, Nynnyaw, and Llevelys. They were all fine men and great warriors, but Lludd and Llevelys exceeded the other two in wisdom. Even as children, the two other brothers came to these two for advice and help. For this reason, when King Beli knew he was about to die, he sent for Lludd and invested him with the kingship of Britain. He chose Lludd over Llevelys because Lludd was older, not because he was wiser. Yet soon after Beli's death, Llevelys got a kingdom of his own. When the king of Gaul died, leaving only a daughter to succeed him, his regent sent an ambassador to Britain asking that one of Beli's sons marry the princess and become king of Gaul. Lludd was happy to choose Llevelys, and Casswallawn and Nynnyaw did

not object, for they were enjoying a war against the Irish in which they were gaining great success and much fine booty. So Lludd ruled in Britain and his brother ruled in Gaul, and so things stood for many years.

But happy times do not last forever, and one day three great evils overtook the British. First there came to the island a group of beings called the Corannyeid. Although they looked human, these creatures were really demons. They immediately began causing all kinds of misfortunes throughout the land, not the least of which was cheating people in business transactions—when they bought something they paid for it with coins that looked real, but that overnight turned to dust, leaving the seller with nothing. When the people of Britain tried to do something about the Corannyeid, they discovered yet another nasty aspect, namely that no matter where or how softly the British spoke, the Corannyeid could hear them talking and so know their plans. Even if two Britons went to the most remote spot on the island and spoke in whispers during a windstorm, the Corannyeid still

heard them. Try as they might, the Britons could never rid themselves of these evil beings because they could never make plans that their unwelcome guests could not overhear and consequently foil.

The second problem was even worse. At times, a loud, piercing shriek would, without warning, rend the peace of the realm. It was so loud that the stained glass windows in the churches would crack, pregnant women would miscarry, and people would temporarily lose their hearing. Try as he might, Lludd could not discover what caused these terrible shrieks, but the uncertainty of when the shrieks would occur caused great concern throughout Britain, and people demanded that King Lludd do something.

The third problem was not as great as the first two, but it was still of great concern to Lludd. Every time Lludd planned a feast, the victuals would be set out the night before, as was the custom, and the next morning everything would have disappeared. No matter how many guards were set over the food, the results were the same. Lludd soon gained the reputation of being a stingy king, and his subjects began to talk among themselves, saying that perhaps they needed a new king.

Now Lludd realized how unhappy his people were and determined that there was only one person in all the world who could help him: his brother Llevelys. He therefore announced that he was going to visit his brother, the king of Gaul, but so as not to arouse the suspicions of the Corannyeid, he told everyone it was a purely social call. Lludd fitted out a fleet that was worthy of the visit of one king to another, and sailed across the Channel to Gaul. When the fleet was still far offshore, Llevelys saw it and joyfully set out in his own royal ship to meet his brother. The two brothers met in the middle of the Channel. Llevelys asked his brother why he had come and Lludd replied in a voice that he knew the Corannyeid could hear that it was a social call. At the same time he signaled his brother for a piece of parchment, on which he briefly wrote a description of his problem and drew a diagram of a long tube that he thought could provide the solution. Without saying a word, Llevelys signaled his men to make the tube.

Once the tube was ready, Lludd put one end in his mouth and signaled for his brother to put the other end in his ear. When this was done Lludd began to speak. But when Lludd spoke into his end, "My brother, I have come to ask your help in solving a great problem that besets my country," Llevelys heard, "You are a poor leader for Gaul and I have come to tell you that your father was not my father but a low-born swineherd." Llevelys yanked the tube from his ear and glared at his brother. "Have you come all this distance just to insult me?" he asked angrily. Bewildered, Lludd spoke again into the tube, "What do you mean, brother? I have come to ask your help!" But all Llevelys heard was his brother calling him a drunken lout. It was a mystery to both brothers, for while each spoke with affection to the other without the tube, any message sent through the tube became corrupted and was certain to raise the anger of one brother toward the other.

Finally Lludd figured it out. "Brother," he said, "I have an idea that a demon is inhabiting this tube. If we pour wine down it, then the demon will flee." This soon proved to be true, for when wine was poured through the tube, the demon fled and the two brothers could talk clearly and, most importantly, without being overheard.

Lludd then explained his problems, and, just as he had expected, his brother had a solution. "Take this bottle full of insects," said Llevelys. "They are a special kind that inhabit the land where the Corannyeid come from. When you get home, kill them and crush them into a fine powder. Mix this powder with water until it is completely dissolved.

A representation of the scene in the myth of Lludd and Llevelys in which Lludd orders the construction of a tube through which he can communicate with his brother Llevelys without the Corannyeid overhearing the conversation. The concept of Llevelys as a king of France and Lludd as a king of Britain is an invention of the later Middle Ages that has been grafted onto the older Celtic legend.

Then call all the people of the kingdom together, including the Corannyeid, for an important announcement. When everyone has gathered together, unstopper the bottle and throw it on the throng. It will do no harm to the normal people, but even the faintest whiff of the mixture will cause the Corannyeid to fall down, writhe in agony, and then die." Lludd thought that was a fine solution and said he would do it. Then he asked his brother if he could help with the second problem.

"Indeed I can," replied Llevelys. "Your kingdom is beset with two dragons that are mortal enemies. The shrieks you hear, brother, are the sounds they make when they fight. To get rid of these beasts you must have your scholars measure the longest distances in your kingdom from north to south and from east to west. Where those two measurements intersect you are to dig a deep pit. In the bottom of that pit you are to place a huge vat of beer—the finest that you can brew in Britain. Then you must cover the vat with a fine silk cloth and wait. The pit and the beer will quickly attract the dragons, for they are curious and great drunkards. Once they both appear at the pit they will begin to fight over the beer in the bottom of the pit, and they will fall, struggling, into the vat. Once they are in the beer they will change into pigs, and at that moment, brother, you must jump down into the pit, draw the four corners of the silk cloth around the pigs, and then have your men pull them out of the pit. Quickly put the pigs and the cloth in a large iron chest and bury the chest as deeply as you can. That will end the problem of the dragons." Lludd liked that idea and told his brother he would do it.

"But can you help me with my third problem? For my subjects think I am a stingy king and do not like to share food with them," said Lludd. And Llevelys told him, "Your problem is a gigantic wizard who owns a magic bag that never becomes full, no matter how much is put into it. Every night, prior to a banquet, this creature comes and stuffs his sack full of your food. He knows a great many spells, one of which can make everyone in your castle fall asleep. When they awake the next morning, everything is gone. When you return to Britain, and after you deal with the first two problems, you must lay out a great feast just as before. But in order that you may resist the spell, have brought from Mount Snowdon ice, and put it into a tub of water so that the water turns icy cold. Throughout the night, as the wizard's spell takes effect, step into the icy tub to wake yourself up. Then when the wizard appears you will be able to kill him easily, for he is not a good fighter and will beg for mercy."

Lludd thanked his brother through the tube and then announced loudly to his retainers that the visit was over and it was time to leave. He boarded his ship, and two days later he was home, ready to put his brother's advice into practice.

First he ground up the insects, dried them, and added water to make a solution. Next, he invited all the people to a meeting. When everyone was there he suddenly threw the water-insect mixture at them. Nothing happened to the Britons, but the Corannyeids fell to the ground writhing in agony and quickly died. The people cheered and declared Lludd the greatest king ever. Thereafter the place where this occurred was called Caer Llundein—Lludd's Castle—a name that has evolved into London.

His first problem solved, Lludd turned to the second problem: ridding Britain of the dragons. His scholars carefully measured the length and breadth of Britain and found that the spot where the line of the longest east-west measurement crossed the line of the longest north-south measurement was near the town of Carmarthen in western Wales. Llevelys dug the pit as instructed and placed

During his conversation with Llevelys, Lludd is told that in order to rid himself of the dragons wreaking havoc in his kingdom, he should dig a deep pit at a certain location and fill the pit with beer, to which the dragons will immediately be attracted. Llevelys tells Lludd that the beasts will fight over the beer, fall into the pit, and be transformed into pigs. The pigs can then be buried in an iron chest and thus vanquished forever. The point at which this pit would have been sited is somewhere near Carmarthen, Wales—the meeting point of a line drawn from the northernmost tip of Scotland, near the Orkneys, to the tip of Cornwall, and another from the easternmost point of land in East Anglia to a point of land west of St. Davids. Dragons are a common element in Welsh mythology, and it is not surprising to find them in Celtic legends.

in it a huge vat of the finest beer. He then covered the vat with a silk cloth. In no time at all, he heard the sound of great leather wings and saw two huge angry dragons descending. They met over the pit and immediately fell to fighting each other. They both tumbled from mid-air into the pit and down into the beer vat, carrying the cloth in with them. Just as his brother had predicted, the vile beasts were transformed into squealing pigs. Lludd jumped down into the pit, grabbed the corners of the cloth, and tied them together. Then he called for his men, who helped him draw the wiggling burden up out of the ground and put it in a great iron chest that they then buried. Lludd was pleased with himself and so were his subjects, who again called him the greatest king ever. He immediately began to prepare for ridding the kingdom of the food-stealing wizard.

He sent runners in relays to bring ice from Mount Snowdon and chilled a great vat of water. He then ordered a great feast laid out on the tables of his banquet hall. Finally, he hid in the shadows and waited. Several times during the night, his eyelids began to droop and he almost fell asleep. Each time this happened, however, he stepped into the vat of ice water and was jolted to full awareness. Finally, just before dawn, a huge man entered the hall carrying a great leather bag. Lludd watched as the man quickly gathered up all the meat and drink off the table and stuffed them into his bag. Lludd was amazed to note that no matter what the wizard put into his sack, it never seemed to expand or to become anywhere near full.

At last, when the wizard had put everything into the bag and was about to leave the banquet hall, Lludd jumped out from behind

A view of Llyn Trawsfynydd, east of Harlech Castle. This area was part of the ancient post-Roman kingdom of Gwynedd, one of the wealthiest Celtic kingdoms in Wales because it controlled the island of Anglesey, where grain was grown in abundance.

a pillar, grabbed a bench, and, swinging it high over his head, brought it firmly down on the wizard's skull. The wizard fell to the floor and Lludd drew his sword for the kill. "Spare me, warrior," cried the wizard. "If I do, what can you do for me, beast?" countered Lludd. "I will replace threefold everything that I have stolen all these months and be your faithful follower from then on," came the reply. Lludd agreed to spare the wizard, and with the surplus food that the sorcerer gave him, he held a feast for every subject in Britain to celebrate freedom from the three terrible things the country had endured for so long. All the people then praised Lludd, saying that he was not only the greatest king the Britons had ever had, but also the greatest king they would ever have.

The dragons do battle before falling into the pit dug by Lludd and being transformed into pigs.

PWYLL LORD OF DYFED AND RHIANNON DAUGHTER OF HERVEYD

Pwyll Lord of Dyfed was a man who keenly pursued the pleasures of the hunt. He had a great pack of hounds that many considered the best in all Wales. One day, when he found that his pack was pursuing a stag in competition with another, strange pack, he became fearful that his dogs would be robbed of the kill. He blew his horn to encourage his dogs to even greater efforts, but as he followed them into a clearing he saw that the other pack had already brought the animal down and was tearing at their kill. Furious, and without thinking about the propriety of his act, he rode his horse into the strange pack, swinging his whip until the dogs fled in terror. His own pack then descended on the kill and began to devour the prize.

He would have been better advised to have used restraint and to have shown a proper regard for the rules of the hunt, for suddenly there burst into the clearing an angry and obviously aristocratic man. Dressed in a green cloak and mounted on a fine horse, this man drew up before Pwyll and demanded, in a voice that was obviously used to being obeyed, "How can you possibly allow your hounds to steal a kill?"

Only then did Pwyll take note of things that he should have noted earlier: the dazzling white color of the hounds and their red ears. These were signs that marked the dogs as creatures from the otherworld. Furthermore, the green cloak of the man marked him as a noble from the same place. Both the man and his hounds, Pwyll now knew, possessed great

magic. For the first time in many years, Pwyll was afraid and regretted his impetuosity. Pwyll bowed respectfully and begged the pardon of this visitor from the otherworld. "How may I win your friendship and make amends for my actions?" asked Pwyll. At first Arawn, for that was the stranger's name, said that nothing could atone for such a churlish act. But he slowly yielded to Pwyll's entreaties and finally named his terms.

His kingdom, it seemed, was threatened constantly by a neighboring king, Havgan, who was a persistent enemy with considerable magical skills. If Pwyll would fight this enemy for Arawn then he and Pwyll could become good friends. Pwyll thought briefly about asking why so powerful a lord as Arawn did not fight Havgan himself, but then, considering his own recent poor behavior, thought better of it. He agreed and asked for the details. Arawn supplied them: "We must switch appearances and places, Pwyll, and you must go and rule my kingdom for a year and I will rule yours for a year. I can easily alter our appearances so that no one will suspect. At the end of that year you will meet Havgan at a ford, not far from here, and hit him. You must knock him off his horse with the first blow. And you must be careful to strike only once, for Havgan possesses great magic and he will regain his strength and power if he is struck more than once. You must remember, only the first blow is mortal."

"I will remember, Lord Arawn," said Pwyll, and with that Arawn brought about the transformation. Soon after, each departed for the other's kingdom.

Pwyll was impressed when he arrived at Annwvyn, Arawn's kingdom. Not only was the kingdom beautiful, the crops bounteous, and the soldiers well trained, but Arawn's queen was the most beautiful and intelligent woman Pwyll had ever met. The first night, Pwyll tried out his new identity at a great ban-

OPPOSITE: Assisted by his page, a medieval knight arms for battle. A Celtic warrior would have worn considerably less armor; in Welsh myths where knights appear in armor of this kind, this is because later storytellers have retold earlier Celtic myths in a contemporary setting.

quet and talked with his retainers and queen; it was a most agreeable time. Finally, it was time for bed and the queen led Pwyll off to the bedchamber without the least suspicion that he was not her husband. Yet once in bed Pwyll did not take advantage of the physical fruits of his transformation, but merely told the lovely queen good night and went to sleep—no doubt leaving the lady in considerable confusion.

When the next morning dawned, Pwyll greeted the queen with affection, and they spent the day in pleasant conversation, during which Pwyll cautiously made inquiries about who was who in the court. He was careful not to arouse the lady's suspicions, and that night they once more went off to the bedchamber after dinner. There, Pwyll honorably turned his face to the wall and did not touch the queen. This behavior continued for the entire year, and while the queen may have been dissatisfied with Pwyll's performance, the rest of the kingdom was not, for he ruled well and wisely. The people prospered and the nobility commented among themselves on the wisdom and intelligence of King Arawn's rule without once suspecting that there had been a switch. The queen, meanwhile, continued to be mystified by her husband's unwelcome celibacy.

At the end of the year, Pwyll announced his intention to go and fight King Havgan. He led his army to the border between Arawn's kingdom and Havgan's and found Havgan there. The battle, if such it can be called, lasted but a moment. Pwyll struck Havgan one mighty blow on his shield and knocked him from his saddle. Havgan begged for another blow, to "finish him" as he said, but Pwyll refused, remembering that an additional blow would restore him to life. The refusal sealed Havgan's fate, and he soon died. Havgan's army subsequently swore allegiance to Arawn and the two kingdoms became one.

With his task completed, Pwyll returned to the clearing in the woods where he had first met Arawn. There the two men exchanged identities and each returned home, curious to find how his kingdom had been ruled in his absence. Both were pleased, for both kingdoms had prospered and no one had suspected the true identities of the two kings. When Arawn discovered that Pwyll had respected the sanctity of the marriage vows for an entire year, he realized what a truly noble person Pwyll was. He also let his queen in on the secret, which probably went a long way toward restoring the woman's confidence in her husband's love for her. From then on, Arawn's kingdom and Pwyll's kingdom were on the best of terms. The kings exchanged visits and gifts, and the two kingdoms assisted each other in war; through this alliance, each kingdom became extremely powerful.

Several years after this adventure, Pwyll Lord of Dyfed went for a walk after dinner with his court. As the party approached a high hill, one of Pwyll's courtiers told him that if a king sat on that hill he would receive either a blow from an invisible fist, indicating that he was not fit to rule, or a vision about the future, to assist him if he was indeed a fit ruler. Pwyll, confident of his capabilities, strode to the top of the hill and sat down. He waited with his retainers and for a time experienced neither blow nor vision. Then, just as the group was beginning to believe that the legend about the hill was false, they saw a beautiful woman on a white horse. Pwyll immediately dispatched a page to ask the identify of the woman. The boy ran after the woman, but the faster he ran, the farther away she got. The page returned, exhausted, to Pwyll. The king immediately dispatched a horseman to apprehend the woman, but he was likewise unable to get close to the mysterious stranger. The next day, however, Pwyll was better prepared. He had his fastest horse

saddled and waiting on the hill, and when the mysterious beauty rode by he jumped into the saddle and set off in pursuit. Yet even his foresight did not help, for the woman kept far ahead of him no matter how fast he drove his horse. In desperation, he cried out for her to wait, and surprise of surprises, she did. He approached, confident that this woman had something to do with his destiny. He asked her where she was going, and she replied that she was seeking Pwyll Lord of Dyfed, for she had a favor to ask him. "Indeed, lady, I am he, and I will grant you any favor you may ask," replied Pwyll.

The woman identified herself as Rhiannon, daughter of Herveyd the Old, and told Pwyll that she would soon be forced to marry a man she did not love, a man named Gwawl mac Clud. Rhiannon hated Gwawl, who was not only stupid but also brooding and sullen. She requested that Pwyll come to her father's court and ask for her hand; Herveyd the Old would grant his wish, she said, for Pwyll was a great king while Gwawl mac Clud was a comparative small fry. Much taken with the woman's beauty, Pwyll agreed to come to her father's court and ask that he be allowed to marry her.

Without delay, Pwyll went to the house of Herveyd the Old, arriving amid all the pomp and splendor that Herveyd could muster, and was ushered into the great hall. He was given the seat of honor and made the lord of the banquet. After being served great amounts of food and wine, Pwyll was about to make his request when a young man, who was blond, handsome, and sullen, made his way into the hall, stood before Pwyll, and said he had a boon to ask of Pwyll. In a half-inebriated state, ignoring the frantic tug on his sleeve from Rhiannon, Pwyll said, "Speak! For I will give you whatever I can."

"I am Gwawl mac Clud," the young man proclaimed, "and I ask that tonight you grant

me permission to marry Rhiannon and proclaim a great wedding feast for my men." Pwyll knew he would have to grant this request because he had given his word, and Rhiannon—who was neither retiring nor bashful—asked him, "What will you do now, you great country clod?" Pwyll told Rhiannon

to hold her tongue, for although he may have been caught off-guard once, he was not without resources and he had thought of a very good plan. Giving Gwawl his most winning grin, Pwyll said, "I cannot give away what is not mine, friend Gwawl, for the food and drink of this feast are not mine to give as they are the gift of Herveyd the Old. But should you return here in a year, I will grant both your wishes."

Later that night, after dinner, Rhiannon asked Pwyll to tell her of his plan. He informed her that he had good relations with the people of the otherworld, whose magic was great, and that they would help him. He was thinking, of course, of Arawn of Annwvyn, who, when Pwyll explained his problem, gave the mortal king a certain magic bag. This bag was small—no bigger than a man's head—but it had the odd characteristic that no matter how much you put into it, it never became full. "I am sure, Lord Pwyll," said Arawn, "that you can find a way to use such a special resource."

"Be assured, King Arawn, that I will find a use for the bag," said Pwyll, who was already hatching a plan.

At the end of the year, right on schedule, Gwawl mac Clud returned to Herveyd's great hall, and Pwyll was ready for him. Pwyll was not in the feast hall when Gwawl arrived. Instead, he had disguised himself as a beggar, and he entered the hall only after the feast was well under way and Gwawl was filled with beer. Pwyll approached the high seat, where Gwawl sat as guest of honor, and said that he came as a suppliant seeking a favor. "And what is that, beggar?" asked Gwawl. "To fill my little bag with food, good lord," replied

In the myth of Pwyll and Rhiannon, Gwawl mac Clud is tricked into a bag by Pwyll and then ingloriously beaten by the king's one hundred retainers. Magic bags and cauldrons frequently play important roles in Celtic myths from both Ireland and Wales.

Pwyll. "Easy, that," laughed Gwawl, and ordered a servant to fill the bag to capacity. Yet no matter how much was put into the bag, it never became full. "What churlish trick is this?" roared Gwawl. "Oh, great Lord," answered Pwyll, trembling as if terrified at his audacity, "the bag cannot be filled until a good and noble man steps into it and begins to stamp down its contents." Immediately Gwawl got up, came down off the high seat, climbed into the bag, and began to stamp on its contents. Pwyll jumped forward and, seizing the bag in one hand and Gwawl's head in the other, pushed the poor, stupid fool deep into the bag and tied it shut. Though he struggled like a champion, Gwawl was unable to break free.

Pwyll, gloating over his victory, added insult to injury by hanging the bag from a rafter and encouraging his retainers to strike the bag with sticks, joking that it was like playing badger-in-the-bag (a Welsh children's game). Since Pwyll had brought nearly one hundred men with him, this proved quite painful. Gwawl, overcome with pain, begged for mercy, stating that this was an undignified death for a person of noble birth. Rhiannon agreed and persuaded Pwyll to release him on the condition that Gwawl accept her marriage to Pwyll and promise not to seek revenge. Gwawl agreed, and Pwyll and Rhiannon celebrated their nuptials at the court of Herveyd the Old, returning afterward to Pwyll's court at Arberth. But this was not the end of their adventures.

After Pwyll and Rhiannon had been married for two years, Pwyll's retainers became worried, for Rhiannon had not produced a male child, or any child for that matter, to carry on the royal line. They went to Pwyll and asked him to take a new wife for the good of the kingdom. Pwyll recognized the legitimacy of their concern but refused the request, asking for an additional year in which to produce an heir. At the end of that time, he promised, if Rhiannon had not produced a fine baby boy, he would divorce her and find another wife. Exactly nine months later, Rhiannon gave birth to a boy. Joyfully, the entire kingdom celebrated the birth. Yet the very first night after the birth, a tragedy struck. The serving women who were charged with caring for mother and child drank a little too much wine, and when they awoke in the morning they discovered that the infant was missing. There was no way to explain the disappearance, and the women knew that they would be severely punished for losing the child.

To escape punishment the servants concocted a cruel plan. First, they killed a puppy and tore it to pieces so that it was unrecognizable as an animal; then they smeared Rhiannon's face with the blood as she slept, and scattered a few bones around the bed. When this was done, they began to scream and tear their hair, wailing that Rhiannon had murdered the infant in the night and eaten it. Certainly, the evidence was convincing, and even poor Rhiannon believed herself guilty of this terrible crime. The women told the court that Rhiannon had awakened during the night, spoken with a voice that was not her own, and—before their very eyes—devoured the baby, reveling as she spread the baby's blood over her body. The court was horrified, and Rhiannon, having no way to deny the story, wanted to kill herself.

She was brought to trial and would have been executed had not Pwyll intervened, out of his love for her, and demanded a lesser sentence. Instead of death, the court determined on a truly humiliating punishment for the noblewoman—for seven years Rhiannon was to sit outside the castle gate at Arberth and recount the story of her crime to anyone who entered; she was also to offer to carry anyone, regardless of his or her station in life, into the castle on her back.

The marriage of Pwyll Lord of Dyfed to Rhiannon, daughter of Herveyd the Old. Rhiannon is the ideal Celtic wife, accepting the dictates of her husband but using her beauty and brains to mold him to her will.

Submitting to her fate, Rhiannon went out through the castle gate, built a small lean-to against the castle wall, and began to suffer her punishment. Everyone coming to Arberth heard her story, and most turned their heads away for the shame of it. Strangely, the people who seemed to revel in her misfortune were the very serving women who had created the tale—they often demanded rides into the castle on the back of their former mistress. So things stood for two years.

At the end of that time, about forty miles (64km) to the east in Gwent Ys Coed, a dependency of King Pwyll's, the local lord, Teirnon, had an adventure that would have an important impact on poor Rhiannon. Lord Teirnon owned a mare, which most people said was the finest in all of Wales, for on May 1 of every year for the last seven years she had given birth to a fine colt. Yet just as regularly for those same seven years, the newborn colt disappeared the night after it was born. These disappearances were a great mystery, and the

wisest men in Wales could not discover the reason. In the eighth year, Teirnon determined to discover what was happening.

After the birth of the newest colt, he hid himself in the stable and waited quietly to see what would happen. Just before dawn, he was startled to see the roof of the building suddenly tilted back by a huge clawed hand with no more effort than a man might use to lift the lid of a box. Then another clawed hand reached through the opening and plucked the colt away from its mother. Without stopping to consider the risk—the hands were huge and belonged to a monster that was certainly many times larger than a man—Teirnon leaped out of his hiding place and swung his great sword, cutting off the hand that held the tiny colt. With a cry of terrible pain, the mutilated stump was jerked back and the roof crashed back down on the stable. Teirnon felt the ground shake as the huge thing ran off roaring with pain. He ran outside the stable and there, to his surprise, he saw seven horses ranging from a yearling to a stallion seven years old that the monster had left behind— these were certainly the horses that had been taken from him in past years. But of more interest to Teirnon was a handsome two-year-old boy with so noble a bearing that Teirnon knew immediately it must be the child of Pwyll and Rhiannon.

The next morning, Teirnon and his retinue set out for Arberth. When they reached the royal castle, they saw Rhiannon sitting at the gate, and as they passed into the courtyard they heard her piteous tale. Teirnon's wife, a kind woman, wanted to stop and release the poor woman from her misery, but Teirnon stopped her, saying, "Woman, only Pwyll can free her. Let us go quickly and tell him." Because the rules of hospitality demanded that Teirnon attend a feast in his honor before discussing business, hours passed before it was proper to tell Pwyll the news.

When Teirnon at last told his tale, Pwyll was overjoyed. They brought the child forward and everyone agreed that the lad must be Pwyll's son, as he had the king's features. Only then did someone remember to summon Rhiannon, who immediately recognized her child, and the family was at last reunited in the happiness they should have been enjoying for two years. Teirnon became a trusted advisor to King Pwyll and foster-father to the boy, who was named Pryderi and grew up to be one of Wales' greatest kings.

BRANWEN
DAUGHTER OF
LLYR

King Bran, also known as "the Raven," ruled well and wisely over all of Britain. Bran was so large that he had never lived in a house because there had never been one big enough to hold him. His advisors were his two brothers, Nissyen and Evissyen. These two had extremely divergent personalities, and when Bran asked their advice he always found that the middle course between their opinions was the best one to follow, for Nissyen always counseled moderation and forgiveness while Evissyen always argued for vengeance and brutality. As a result, Bran gained the reputation of being the wisest king in Europe, but his two brothers hated each other because it seemed they were always in competition.

One day when King Bran, Nissyen, and the members of the court were sitting on the high hill at Harlech in northern Wales, they saw a huge fleet coming toward them from the direction of Ireland. The ships in this fleet were well fitted-out and each carried a shield tied to the mast just under the yardarm to announce that theirs was a peaceful mission.

OPPOSITE: Caerphilly Castle, Glanmorgan, Wales, near Cardiff. Wales has always been the focus of much warfare, and security often depended on a strong castle. Caerphilly Castle was built on the river Taff to protect the approaches to Cardiff Castle, seven miles to the south. This castle stands on an earlier Celtic fortification.

Branwen White Breasts, sister of King Bran of Wales, meets her future husband, King Mallolwch of Ireland. The conflict between the Welsh and the Irish that resulted from this marriage is probably a vague recollection, on the part of the author of *The Mabinogion*, of an ancient raid on Gwynedd by the Irish.

King Bran immediately sent messengers to the landing to ask to whom this grand fleet belonged and to bid them welcome. He found that the fleet was that of King Mallolwch of Ireland, who had come to ask for the hand of King Bran's sister, Branwen White Breasts, in marriage. King Bran was happy to hear this and so was Nissyen, who advised the king to accept, for this would create a firm alliance between two powerful countries. Evissyen was not there, but Bran felt that his brother could not possibly object to so fine a match.

Bran ordered a great feast, and many men made many fine speeches. The eating and drinking lasted all night and into the next morning. Happily, King Mallolwch was much taken with Branwen, and she with him.

Everything would have been fine if it had not been for Evissyen, who, on his return, took exception to King Bran's decision to allow the marriage. Secretly, Evissyen thought the marriage was a fine idea, but he nonetheless raised many objections to it, for he was angered that Bran had made the decision without asking his advice. When Bran would not change his mind, Evissyen set out to ruin the arrangement.

He sneaked off to the stable where King Mallolwch had stabled his horses and mutilated the poor animals with a knife. He cut away the lips of the poor beasts so that their teeth showed, cut their ears off, and peeled back their eyelids so the animals could not blink. When Mallolwch found his horses so brutally maimed, he had to kill them, and he swore to leave Wales immediately and seek vengeance on his Welsh hosts. He did marvel, however, that a people who had feted him and betrothed a princess to him in the same day could turn around and insult him the next day.

King Bran did not want the Irish to leave, and he sent a delegation to Mallolwch to persuade him to stay. The delegation apologized and swore to pay compensation: to each man whose horse had been maimed, a finer horse than the one that had been lost, and for King Mallolwch, a rod of silver as tall as a man and a plate of gold as big around as the king's face. As further incentive to peace, Bran offered Mallolwch a huge, magical iron cauldron that had the power to raise the dead; when a man was killed in battle and afterward thrown into this cauldron, he immediately emerged completely healed save that he had lost his power of speech. This was a truly valuable item for a king and Mallolwch forgot his anger and asked Bran how he had gotten the cauldron, for he had once seen one just like it. Bran replied, "Indeed you have, sire; it is probably the very one, for I got it from two people who came originally from Ireland, Llassar Llaes Gyngwyd and his wife, Kymidei Kymeinvoll."

"Indeed I know those two, King Bran," replied Mallolwch, "for I once had them as guests, and a dirtier, viler pair have never yet been born. The man, Llassar Llaes Gyngwyd, was a braggart and a drunk, and the woman was a lustful slut who attempted to seduce my nobles although none would lie with her because of her stench and foul breath."

"Then," asked King Bran, "why did you let them stay with you?"

"Because they were too big and too dangerous to force out easily, and because the woman gives birth every six weeks to a fully armed and fully grown warrior. I tolerated them so that I could build up my army. Indeed, three of her spawn are with me now." And Mallolwch pointed out the window to three monstrous creatures who were as tall as trees and as broad as walls and looked exactly alike. The king went on to tell Bran that only when his subjects threatened to revolt and topple him from his throne did he get rid of Llassar and Kymidei.

Mallolwch had ordered that an enormous house be built out of iron plates and the metal covered with wood so that the structure resembled a feast hall. He had then invited the two monsters to a grand feast, and when they were both thoroughly satiated with food and besotted with beer, the other feasters sneaked away, the doors were barred, and the servants kindled a great fire around the base of the structure so that it was soon an oven and the two unwelcome guests were the bread. Llassar and his wife began to bellow like bulls and throw themselves against the walls, trying to break them down. At first the walls were too strong, but then, as they grew white-hot and became weakened, Llassar seized the great cauldron, placed it on top of his head, and ran like a battering ram against the wall. He crashed through and Kymidei followed him. Both emerged singed and smoking, and they ran straight to the Irish Sea to cool themselves off. Then, using the cauldron as a boat, they paddled across the sea to Wales.

King Bran laughed and took up the tale. "I remember their arrival well. They were impressed with my great size and also seemed subdued by their harsh treatment in Ireland. They agreed to live quietly in the hills behind Harlech and produce a new soldier for my army every six weeks if I would supply them with food and shelter." And Bran summoned six monstrous soldiers who were the result of this arrangement and sent them out to visit with their Irish brothers.

The promise of new horses, King Bran's personal gifts of silver and gold to King Mallolwch, and the pleasant and humorous conversation about their similar experiences with Llassar Llaes Gyngwyd and Kymidei Kymeinvoll had a good effect on the Irish king,

The armor worn by this mounted knight is a classic example of mid-fifteenth-century armor. By this time, armor had evolved as a result of the advent of the longbow and the development of firearms.

and he agreed to forget about the insult of Evissyen. However, while their king was willing to forget, many Irish nobles were not, and they continued, whenever they could, to urge their king to take vengeance in some way. King Mallolwch, however, was influenced by Branwen's great beauty and, by the time he had returned to Ireland, was much in love with her. In no time at all, Branwen had become pregnant, and she soon gave birth to a beautiful boy who was named Gwern.

But Mallowch's ardor cooled in three years, and the manipulations of those Irish who still sought vengeance on the Welsh fi-

nally had its effect. The king began to take other women into his bed, and finally banished the lovely Branwen to the royal kitchens as a pot scrubber. Yet he feared the anger of Bran should the Welsh king find out about this insult to his sister, so he forbade ships to sail from Ireland to any port in Britain, lest word of Branwen's disgrace get out.

Branwen, however, was not the type of woman to accept this situation. She had befriended a young starling that had fallen from its nest and, partially out of loneliness but also with a goal of getting word to her brother, had taught the bird to speak. When she could communicate with the animal, she told it the whole story and begged it to fly across the sea and tell her brother. The bird, out of love, agreed to go, and it flew straight to King Bran. He was angry beyond words and ordered an immediate attack on the Irish for this great insult. For once, both Nissyen and Evissyen agreed that this was the right thing to do. The Welsh fleet set sail in such force that it covered the water. King Bran himself was too large to fit in a boat, so he waded along beside his ships, bearing his harpists and skilled workmen on his shoulders.

As the fleet neared the coast of Ireland, one of King Mallolwch's soldiers caught sight of it in the twilight. The size of the fleet and the near-darkness prevented the man from identifying it exactly, and he reported only that he had seen something monstrous coming toward the coast. When the king questioned him closely, the man said it seemed that a whole forest was moving toward the coast, and that it appeared that in the midst of that forest there was a high ridge with a large pool of water on either side of it. King Mallolwch realized that this could not be, and asked his wise men to try to figure out what the soldier had really seen. They could not, but one of them remembered Branwen down in the kitchen and told the king to send for

In addition to bulls, the ancient Celts venerated horses as a sign of status. Hundreds of representations of horses survive in Celtic art. This bronze abstract rendering of a horse, now in the British Museum, London, measures about four inches (10cm) high. It was probably originally created to adorn a shield.

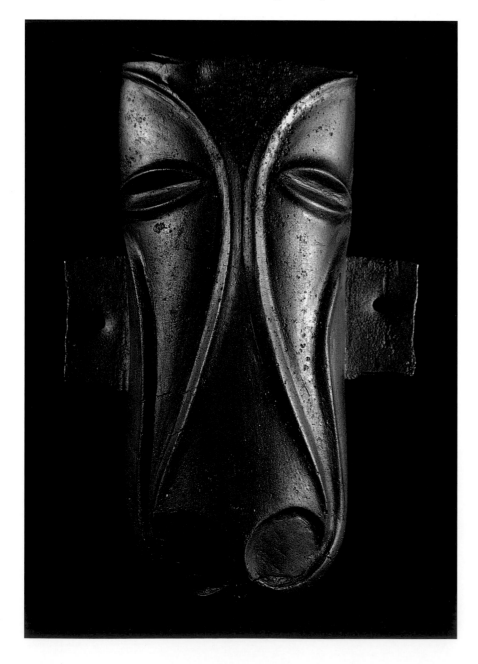

his exiled wife, "for if this thing is coming from Wales, she might know what it is."

Branwen was dragged, sweaty and disheveled, from her station at the cooking fires. Although she was covered in grime, it was clear that a year in the kitchens had not diminished her beauty in the slightest. She drew herself up—every inch the queen—and demanded why she had been so unceremoniously summoned from her work. When Mallolwch described the stange phenomenon off the coast, Branwen clapped her hands and laughed. "Now, woman beater, you will see the might of the Welsh come to avenge my treatment, for the forest your man thought he saw was really the many masts of my brother's fleet gathered so thickly together on the water that they seem like a forest. The ridge with the lakes on either side was merely my brother's huge face, for the ridge is his nose and the lakes his giant blue eyes. Poor Mallolwch, you should fear for your kingdom."

Mallolwch called his warriors together and asked for advice. They were proud of their fighting ability, but they also feared the numbers of the Welsh and the great size of Bran. After hours of discussion and argument, they decided to withdraw across the River Liffy, destroy the bridge, and attempt to hold the Welsh at the river. The strategy seemed to work at first, for when the Welsh attempted to cross the river, their boats were swept out to sea by the swift current.

When Bran saw that his troops were having problems, he donned a thick helmet, slung a shield across his back, and threw himself face-down across the river so that his feet were resting on one side and his helmeted

King Bran of Gwynedd strides through the Irish Sea as he accompanies his invasion fleet to Ireland. Kings, heros, and villains of great size are a common feature of many Celtic myths.

head on the other. In this way, he formed a bridge over which his troops swarmed to fight the Irish. To this day the site of this amazing event is called Baile Atha Cliath—Toward the Hurdle Ford—for it was there that Bran helped his men hurdle the ford. This spot is now known as Dublin.

When King Mallolwch saw that his army was in danger of being defeated, he decided to try trickery. He tempted Bran with an offer to negotiate in a house large enough for Bran to sit in. In all his life Bran had never sat under a roof, and it was an experience he dearly craved; so when the Irish made the offer, Bran jumped at the chance. King Mallolwch put his workmen to building a huge house, lavishing great care and sparing no expense on its decorations. But he also determined to use the house to get the better of King Bran. His workmen hung a bag from each of the hundred posts that held up the roof. Inside each bag was a fully armed warrior who, on signal, was to jump out and attack the Welsh when they

had drunk too much beer. But Mallolwch figured without the suspicions of Evissyen, who
was as bitter and distrustful as ever.

Before Bran entered the hall, Evissyen
went to inspect it. Carefully looking over the
arrangements, he saw one of the bags move.
He felt one and realized that each bag held a
man. He did not make public his discovery,
but instead asked one of the Irish workers
what was in them. "Nothing, Lord," replied
the man, "save flour."

Evissyen nodded, stuck his hand in the
bag, felt for a head, and crushed it so that the
man in the bag died quickly and without a
sound. Then Evissyen went to the next bag
and did the same, repeating this action until
he had killed the inhabitant of each bag.
What were the Irish workers to do? To shout a
warning would only get them killed, so they
stood quietly by while Evissyen did his work.

Shortly after Evissyen finished, the two
kings arrived. There followed a feast during
which the two expressed the greatest love for

each other and swore to maintain eternal
friendship. Mallolwch even brought
Branwen from the kitchen, dressed
in the finest clothing, to assure
Bran that all was well. But lest
Bran be fooled, Evissyen whis-
pered into his ear, telling him about
the men in the bags and showing
the king how treacherous the Irish
were. However, Nissyen, the
brother who always spoke for forgiveness, encouraged Bran to accept peace. So convincing was
Nissyen that Bran finally relented.
Evissyen seemed to accept this and
said, "King, let us cement this
friendship by agreeing to allow
Gwern, the son of Branwen and
Mallolwch, to be designated king
of Ireland when Mallolwch dies.
Call the boy forth to invest him."

Mallolwch accepted this offer and called
Gwern forth. But as Gwern passed by Evissyen, the royal advisor suddenly grabbed the
boy by the feet, swinging him up and around
his head, and threw the lad head-first into the
fire. The child landed on a stone, his head
cracked open, and his brains spilled out and
were cooked on the hot stones.

Amazed at this treachery, the Irish sprang
to arms and began to fight, thinking that their
countrymen in the bags would come to their
aid. But they soon realized the "bag men"
were not coming and that they were greatly
outnumbered. The battle in the huge house
swayed back and forth, and the Irish sent for
reinforcements. Outside, they kindled a fire
under their magic cauldron, filled it with water, and prepared to use its magical properties
to restore their casualties. The British killed
many more of the Irish than they lost, but the
Irish used their magic cauldron to keep returning the recently killed to battle. When
Evissyen noted that he had just killed a man

for the second time, he realized what the Irish were doing. He fought his way to the cauldron, jumped in, and, bracing his feet against one side, pushed with all his strength against the sides of the vessel. The vessel cracked and broke into two parts, ruined. Unfortunately for Evissyen, the exertion broke his heart and he finally paid for the duplicity that had led to this situation in the first place.

With their reanimated reinforcements gone, the Irish army dwindled until all were killed. On the British side, however, the losses were also great, and by the end of the battle only seven Welsh soldiers remained of the great invasion force that had entered Ireland. Even Bran died, after he was wounded with a poisoned arrow. He realized he was dying and called the seven survivors to his side to extract a promise from them. They were to cut off his head and carry it to London, where they were to bury it on the White Hill, with the face toward France. With the foresight that was common to Welsh kings, he predicted it would take his seven friends eighty-seven years to accomplish this task, for there would be various delays on the way.

The seven immediately set out with the severed head, but stopped at Harlech, where they stayed for seven years feasting, drinking, and bragging about their adventures in Ireland. Next they went to Pembroke in Cornwall, England, where they spent eighty years at the castle of a hospitable king. Miraculously, the head remained uncorrupted all this time and spoke to its companions several times to add to the tales they told of the great battle in Ireland and to remind them to get on with their task. At the end of eighty years the head convinced them, and they finally took it all the way to London and buried it in a great ceremony. As long as the head remained buried, London was free of the plague; however, when William the Conqueror had the foundations dug for his great tower in London, his workers dug up the head, and London has suffered intermittently from terrible plagues and diseases ever since.

In Ireland, at the end of the battle only five pregnant women had survived the slaughter, by hiding in a cave. All five bore sons. When they grew up, each of the sons took another man's mother as wife and so produced yet another set of children, so that today everyone in Ireland is descended from these five women.

GEREINT AND ENID

Once, when Arthur, king of Britain, held court at Caer Llion ar Wysg (modern Cardiff), his forester, Madawg mac Twrgadarn, who was responsible for guarding the king's lands in the Forest of Dean, came to Arthur with an announcement. Madawg had seen a wondrous deer, pure white, proud, and fleeter than any animal he had ever seen. Arthur decided that he and his whole court would go on a hunt the next morning. His wife, Gwenhwyvar, and all her court ladies would accompany him.

The next morning, however, Gwenhwyvar was in such a deep sleep and looked so peaceful that Arthur could not bear to wake her, so he went on the hunt without her. When the beautiful queen awoke she was angry, for she loved the thrill of the hunt more than anyone else did. She summoned her ladies-in-waiting and sent one of them to get horses for them all. But the woman returned with the news that the grooms, thinking no one else was going hunting that morning, had let all but two of the horses out into the fields. Gwenhwyvar feared that if they waited for the horses to be gathered from the pasture they would never catch the hunters, so she ordered the two available horses saddled and set out.

An idealized King Arthur in late-medieval armor. The figure of Arthur extends back into the fifth century A.D., when he was depicted as a hero of the Britons. When these myths were written down, he was changed from a valiant hero to a great and celebrated king. In reality, Arthur was probably not a king, but a successful Celtic warrior who won critical battles at a time when victory was essential to the fortunes of the Celts in Britain.

Cardiff Castle, Cardiff, Wales. There has always been some kind of fortification at Cardiff to protect the natural harbor where the Taff River flows into Bristol Channel. The current castle was begun in the eleventh century, but has been modified numerous times since then. The front part of the castle dates from the eighteenth century, while the towers behind it were built in the thirteenth century.

The two women rode through the woods following the distant sound of the hunt's horns. They set a fast pace but, try as they might, could not catch the hunting party. As they rested beside a brook, a young nobleman came upon them. Gwenhwyvar clapped her hands joyfully, for the young man was Gereint, the most handsome man at court and a clever and interesting conversationalist. At least the ride through the forest would not be boring. She asked Gereint to accompany her and her companion, and the three set out to find Arthur.

No sooner had they started off, however, than they suddenly came upon an unknown knight in full armor armed with a lance and accompanied by a dwarf and a maiden. As was customary, Gwenhwyvar sent her lady-in-waiting forward to ask the name of the knight, but no sooner had the lady asked her question than the dwarf sneered, "Such a lowly person as yourself is not fit to know the name of so noble a knight." And with that, he struck the poor woman across the face with his riding crop, leaving her with a wicked red welt. She returned in tears. Gereint, angry at this treatment, rode up and demanded the meaning of such an act; the dwarf, however, did not answer but struck him across the face as well. Then the strange knight and his party rode quickly off.

Drawing his sword, Gereint moved to attack the knight, but Gwenhwyvar, as practical as she was beautiful, ordered him to sheathe his sword. "Sir knight," she said, "you are without armor. To attack that knight, who is in full battle dress, would be foolhardy. I beg you to reconsider, and wait until you are like-wise armed." Gereint realized Gwenhwyvar's wisdom and put up his sword. He asked the queen and her lady to return to court to dress the poor lady's wound, while he followed the knight to learn his name.

All day Gereint followed the knight through the woods, until he arrived at a town. The strange knight entered the gates of the town and was welcomed by the guard. Gereint also entered the town, thinking that here was an opportunity to search for infor-mation. He wandered the streets making dis-creet inquiries until he came to a ruined building in front of which there sat an old man dressed in the most ragged clothes Gereint had ever seen. Despite his dress, though, the fellow had a dignified bearing, and Gereint asked him if he knew the strange knight who had entered the town. "Indeed I do, warrior," said the old man, whose name was Niwl. "Come home with me and I will tell you all you need to know."

So Gereint followed the man home, and there the knight met Niwl's daughter, Enid, who was as ragged as her father but was a beautiful woman nonetheless. She was also quite cheerful and full of information about the town and the people in it—she knew all about the mysterious knight. His name was Edern son of Nudd and he was a famous and skilled knight, if a little arrogant. "He has come, sir knight," said Enid, "to be in the tournament tomorrow. Every year, the local earl holds a joust. Edern has entered for the last two years and has always won. If he wins again this year, he will keep forever the great trophy cup that is the prize."

"How may I enter that tournament?" asked Gereint. "And how may I get some ar-mor, lady?"

"No knight may enter the tournament unless he has a lady in whose honor he fights. He must dedicate the prize to her and swear to serve her forever," replied Enid.

"Then, maiden, if you will be my lady and let me enter the tournament on your be-half tomorrow, I promise that if I win you will be my wife."

Enid accepted and Niwl lent Gereint his old and rusted armor, for the old man had once been a young and restless knight. Indeed, he had been lord of all the land around—as Gereint heard that night at din-ner—but had lost it to the present earl by force of arms.

The next morning, Gereint, Niwl, and Enid went to the tournament field. Gereint looked ridiculous in his rusted armor, and everybody laughed at the rusty knight, the

An array of swords and armor, including (at upper left) an upper arm protector called a pauldron. To facilitate easy movement of the arm, pauldrons had overlapping layers of metal called epaulieres. The spiked elbow piece was called a coudiere, and was designed so that a knight could deliver a lethal backward blow with his arm.

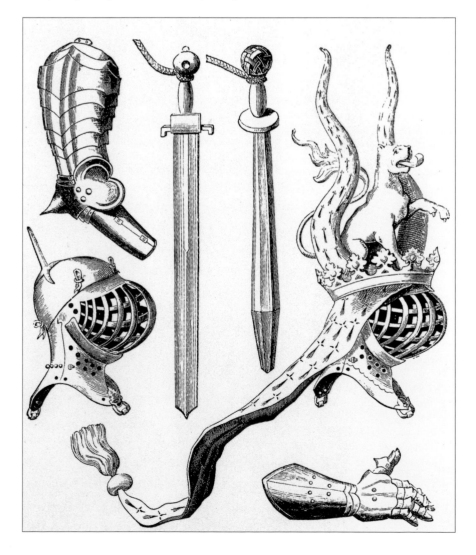

ragged old man, and the young and equally ragged girl. But once Gereint began to joust, people forgot to laugh and instead were thrilled by his skill. Gereint unhorsed six knights in a row, and then, after a short rest, six more. Finally, the only knight left on the field was the mysterious warrior who had insulted Gereint and Gwenhwyvar's lady-in-waiting. The two went to opposite ends of the field and rode toward each other furiously. Twice, each splintered his lance on the other's shield. Finally, Niwl handed Gereint a lance that had been his as a youth and that had never splintered, no matter how hard he had ridden at an enemy. Armed with this lance, Gereint hit the other knight's shield right in the center, breaking it in half. Edern tumbled from the saddle. Gereint jumped off his mount, and the two men began to hack and slash at each other until their armor was bent and broken in a hundred places. Finally, Gereint succeeded in battering Edern to the ground, and Edern begged for mercy. Gereint granted mercy on the condition that Edern travel to Caer Llion ar Wysg and beg the forgiveness of Gwenhwyvar for the blow his dwarf had given her lady-in-waiting.

Within minutes of Gereint's victory, the local earl came onto the field. He congratulated Gereint on his victory and begged him to come to dinner. Remembering the hospitality of Niwl, however, Gereint replied that he already had an invitation to dinner. Yet when Niwl, Enid, and Gereint returned to Niwl's humble house, they were surprised to see servants and slaves bringing food, tables, chairs, and rich wine to Niwl's house. The earl had decided that if Gereint would not come to dinner with him, he would bring dinner to Gereint. Over dinner that night, the earl, still impressed with Gereint's skill at arms, asked if he could give him anything. "I will give you anything that is in my power to give, knight, up to half my lands." Then Gereint said to him, "If that is true, and I do not doubt it, for you seem a man of honor, then return half of your lands to Niwl, the man from whom you took them, and give him a retinue of men-at-arms to defend them." The earl, a good-natured fellow at heart, laughed at his own foolish generosity and granted Gereint his wish. That taken care of, Gereint and Enid left the next morning for Caer Llion ar Wysg and the court of Arthur.

His arrival was expected, for Edern had taken Gereint's injunction literally and had made as rapid a journey as possible to the court of King Arthur. In fact, at the very moment that Gereint was demanding that the earl give part of his land to Niwl, Edern was begging Gwenhwyvar to forgive him. She, kind woman that she was, granted forgiveness on the condition of a year's good service to herself and her ladies.

The next morning, Arthur, having heard Edern's story, laid out the best spread he could in anticipation of Gereint's arrival, and the young knight received a hero's welcome. Arthur then "married" Gereint and Enid (there was no formal marriage in Celtic society), and Queen Gwenhwyvar and her ladies immediately took Enid under their collective wing and whisked her away to dress her in finery and prepare her for court. Enid's pleasant nature and her husband's military skills soon made them the most popular young couple at Caer Llion ar Wysg.

For the next year, Gereint fought in tournaments all over Britain, and he always won. All the while, his love and admiration for Enid grew and grew. But by the beginning of the next year, his love of Enid had begun to bring him trouble.

Because he won every tournament he fought, Gereint started to become bored with fighting altogether, and turned to the other great love of his life—Enid—with whom he never became bored. Gradually, he began to

spend much more time with her than with the other warriors at court. In the intensely male-dominated world of Arthur's court, forsaking the company of men for that of a woman, no matter how charming and beautiful, was sure to bring criticism. Edern, who was still at court, heard these criticisms and spoke to Enid about it. She was, of course, concerned, for no woman likes to see her man lose face with his peers. Yet she was afraid to

mention her concern to Gereint for fear of his anger, and her anxiety increased until one morning, as Gereint slept, she began to cry.

Her sobbing awakened Gereint and she was forced to tell him what she had heard. Uncharacteristically and illogically, Gereint became angry with Enid. He roared at the trembling woman that his fighting ability was as sharp as ever and that he would prove it that day. "We will go into the forest together, but you will ride ahead of me. On no account are you to warn me of danger. I am equal to whatever I may meet, and you will soon see that I have not lost my fighting prowess." And so the two left Caer Llion ar Wysg and went into the deepest part of the woods.

In no time at all Enid saw four strange knights approaching. Because she had never seen them before, she knew they were not the king's men, but young, unattached knights eager to build a reputation—the most dangerous and aggressive kind. She saw the danger of four against one, weighed what Gereint had said about not warning him of danger, and, deciding that there was a good chance that these four might kill Gereint if they attacked without warning, rode back to tell him of their approach. Gereint was angry and began to curse the poor girl, but had to break off quickly and defend himself, for suddenly the four knights appeared, riding down the hillside at full gallop.

In short order, and seemingly without effort, he knocked two of the knights off their horses with such force that they were dead before they hit the ground. The next two war-

riors renewed their attack with extra vigor, but Gereint also knocked them off their horses. These two still had fight left in them, and Gereint had to dismount and finish them off with sword strokes. Once he had vanquished them, Gereint turned his anger on Enid, threatening her with a beating if she warned him of danger again. He then loaded all the armor of the four knights onto one of the dead men's horses, and instructed Enid to lead this horse, as well as the other three, after her. Gereint hoped that the horses and the armor would serve as a lure, tempting other knights to try and take them so that he would again have an opportunity to prove that he was still a virile man and a valiant warrior.

Within a few miles, Enid saw three more knights approaching. "Here are some easy pickings," said one of the strange knights loudly, "four suits of armor, four horses, and a young girl for our pleasure." All three knights spurred their mounts toward Enid. The poor girl now suffered quite a dilemma: the man she loved was in danger, for he was already exhausted from his previous fight and could not, she thought, possibly take on another three knights, especially if they surprised him. Still, she had been promised a beating if she warned him again. Nonetheless, so great was her love that she decided she would rather be beaten by the man she loved than see him killed, so she turned her horse around and rode back to warn him.

Instead of thanking her, Gereint glared angrily at her and rode forward to do battle. As he charged forward, he knocked the lance of the first knight aside and, without stopping, hit the second knight squarely in the chest—the knight was dead before he touched the ground. Gereint did not pause but went straight on for the third knight, knocking him off his horse as well. Jumping down off his horse, Gereint slew that knight with his sword and then coolly killed the first knight, who

Two knights fighting on foot. Both knights wear a helmet called a salade. The salade was not attached to the suit of armor, but was designed to cover the top two-thirds of the head. Being un-attached, it allowed wider freedom of movement and was much cooler. The jaw and lower face of a knight wearing a salade was generally protected by a metal attachment called a mentonniere.

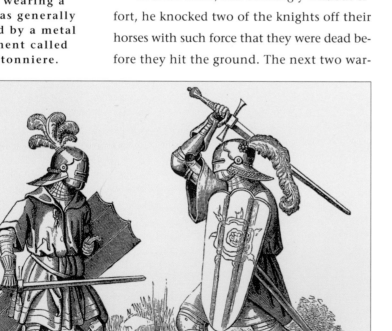

was still groggy from Gereint's first blow. Poor Enid now sat silently and fearfully on her horse, expecting to be beaten. But Gereint only abused her with words and ordered her back to her position far in front of him with three more horses and three more suits of armor as a temptation for the next group of wandering knights. "Heed my words and say nothing to me even if all hell come against me, for I am equal to them in battle."

Soon the little cavalcade of two people, eight suits of armor, and nine horses was spotted by a group of five knights. Enid, far in advance, heard one of them say, "This is surely a rich prize for us! All that armor and horseflesh plus a girl to share; and guarded by only one sorry-looking knight." Enid, still willing to accept blows to save the man she loved, turned back toward Gereint and told him what she had heard. Gereint said only that she would live to hate the fact that she had broken silence, and then rode off to confront the five knights. Despite her greatest fears, he quickly and expertly killed them all.

These rounds of battles, threats, and the accumulation of additional suits of armor continued through nine more conflicts. Even though he was always outnumbered, Gereint always won, and his physical ability and stamina amazed Enid, who realized the truly astonishing ability of her lover and finally realized that he had no need of warnings from her or anyone else. But even Gereint overreached himself. Late in the day, he encountered a man sitting by the side of the road whose lord had been slain by three eighteen-foot (5.4m) giants armed with clubs the size of full-grown oak trees. Gereint questioned

Enid comforts the dying Gereint, who, through the power of love, would soon live again. Note the boar crest on the helmet. Boars were a sign of high rank in Celtic society, probably derived from the tradition of the hero's portion at Celtic feasts.

the man and promised to exact vengeance for this murder. He pursued the beasts and, after a fierce fight, slew all three. But the effort was too much for him. He rode back to Enid, fell from his horse, and died in her arms.

Overcome with grief, Enid cried, moaned, and tore her hair until the noise attracted a passing knight, Earl Limwris, who upon seeing Enid decided to rape her. Oblivious to her screams and unsuccessful attempts to defend herself, he began to tear the clothes from the poor girl; he was just about to have his way with her when Gereint awoke from the dead. Enid's plight and her pure, unadulterated, all-sacrificing love had brought him back to life. He jumped up, drew his sword, and made short work of Limwris.

And it was only then that Gereint realized the overwhelming love that Enid had for him—so powerful that it raised him from the dead to defend her. He finally forgave her, and from that day forward he never again doubted her love for him.

FROM CELTIC HEROES TO CHRISTIAN SAINTS

While Christianity helped preserve Celtic mythology—albeit in an altered form—it also incorporated or adapted mythological stories as miraculous events in the lives of Celtic saints. Certainly, Christian saints could not excel in battle, but they could carry on the mythological genre within a framework of miracles performed to propagate the faith.

Saint Patrick (A.D. 390–461), the most important Irish saint, not surprisingly had the greatest numbers of miracles associated with him. Many of these

St. Patrick, the patron saint of Ireland, was born to an aristocratic family in Strathclyde, an early Celtic kingdom that consisted of portions of modern-day southern Scotland and northwestern England.

have to do with Patrick's struggle with the Druids, for these religious leaders had a great deal to lose if Christianity took root.

When Patrick first came to the court of King Loeguire, the High King of Ireland, two Druids, Lochru and Lucetmail, disputed his preaching. After Patrick endured their insults for a time, he prayed to God for help and begged that Lochru, the most obnoxious of the two, might die. No sooner had the last syllable left Patrick's mouth than a mysterious force lifted poor Lochru high into the air and dropped him head-first to the ground, where his skull burst open on a rock and his brains dripped out. The description of this mortal wound calls to mind some of the injuries inflicted by Cuchulainn on his Connacht enemies during the Tain Bo Cuailnge.

Later, Patrick performed less lethal deeds. When the Druid Lucetmail challenged Patrick to make it snow, Patrick refused, saying that he could not do what was contrary to nature. With a sneer, Lucetmail created a heavy snow that piled up to the hubs of the chariot wheels. Now Patrick showed his mettle; he raised his hand and, with a mere wave, caused all the snow to vanish. It might have been contrary to nature for it to snow in Ireland in April, Patrick explained to the king, but it was in concert with nature to clear snow away.

Next, Lucetmail brought darkness over the area at noontime. But Patrick swept this away, again with a wave of the hand, explaining to the amazed court that the Druids could work only evil, but the greatness of Christianity was that it worked magic only for good.

Finally, Patrick proposed a test of the relative power of the Druids and the Christians. He had a group of workmen construct a house, one half of which they built out of green wood and the other half out of dry wood. Then he told one of his disciples to exchange clothing with one of Lucetmail's followers. Patrick's disciple, dressed as a Druid, went and stood in the part of the house built of dry wood, while Lucetmail's disciple, dressed as a Christian, stood in the green-wood part of the house. When all was ready, Lucetmail himself set the house on fire. To the amazement of all, the Druid burned up, while Patrick's disciple emerged unharmed from the fire. Turning to the court, Patrick said, "You have seen the power of the Lord at work. I ask you to believe in the Lord Christ, or God will

destroy you all." Not surprisingly, King Loeguire and his entire court asked Patrick to baptize them right then and there.

Many of the myths of the early Celtic saints involved their power over animals. Saint Ciaran of Clonmacnoise (515–545) trained a fox to carry his copy of the Psalms, and when the fox yielded to its hunger and ate the book for its leather binding, Ciaran forgave the animal and saved it from his angry followers. Because Ciaran had been merciful, God restored the partially eaten Psalter to its original condition.

Saint Kevin of Glendalough once dropped his copy of the Psalms into a deep lake. He asked an otter to dive for the book, and the otter did so. Later, Kevin trained the animal to catch salmon each day and bring the fish to the monastic kitchen.

The most famous example of the Celtic saints' power over animals involved Saint Columba of Iona (521–597) and the Loch Ness monster. In 586, Columba went to Scotland to try to convert the fierce Picts under King Brud. On the way, he and his followers came to the southern shore of Loch Ness and wanted to cross at a point where a rope was set to draw a small boat across the loch. Unfortunately, they arrived just in time to see a huge monster surface near the boat as it came across the loch, frighten the poor boatman

ABOVE: St. Kevin's Church and Round Tower, County Wicklow, Ireland. During the Viking raids on Ireland, the Irish monks built protective structures in the form of high, round towers that were difficult for the Vikings to take without siege equipment.

RIGHT: Loch Ailsh, Durnie, Scotland. The dark and mysterious waters of the Scottich lochs, colored black by the peat that constantly seeps into them from the surrounding soil, naturally give rise to legends and tales of monsters. The castle in the foreground is Eilean Donan.

out of the boat, and swallow the man. Without the least hesitation, Columba ordered one of his disciples to swim across the loch to get the small boat and bring it back so that he and his followers could cross. The man jumped into the water and started to swim for the boat. The monster, attracted by the swimmer, turned to attack him, but Columba, with a mere wave of his hand, caused the creature to submerge and leave the man alone. Columba's disciple then brought the boat back, and the future saint and his whole group crossed the loch in perfect safety. When word of this encounter with the monster reached King Brud and his court, the king ordered all his people to accept baptism from the saint's hand. This, by the way, is the first written reference to the monster that has fascinated both saints and sinners ever since.

PRONUNCIATION OF CELTIC WORDS AND NAMES

Celtic words and names are difficult both to spell and to pronounce, even for scholars. Very little is known of the ancient pronunciation, and certain words have changed through transliteration and habitual mispronunciation (Tara, for instance, was originally spelled Teamhair, which would have been pronounced "t'yower"). Despite all this, there do exist certain guidelines that should enable modern readers to come close to the correct pronunciation of the various Celtic words and names in this book. Generally speaking, -dd is pronounced "-th," -ll is rendered as "-hl," and -mh and -bh are pronounced "-v"; the letter c is always hard (pronounced "k"); and -ch is breathed, as in the Scottish loch ("lake"). Below are the pronunciations of some of the more common terms and names from the book (capital letters indicate the stressed syllable).

Ailill	AL-ill
Annwvyn	an-NOO-vin
caer	ker
Cernunnos	KER-noo-nohss
Cian	KEE-an
Conchobar	CON-ah-khar
Cuailnge	COO-lee
Cuchulainn	coo-HOOL-in
Dyfed	DUF-it (or DUV-it)
Emain	EV-in
Gwawl	GOO-owl
Gwenhwyvar	GWIN-hwee-var
Llevelys	hlev-ELL-iss
Lludd	hlooth
Lugh	loo
Magh Tuiredh	moy TOO-rah
Mallolwch	ma-HLOL-lukh
Miodhchaoin	MEE-than
Niamh	NEE-ahv
Samhain	SHAH-vin
sidh	shee
tain	tahn
Tuatha de Danu	TOO-tha day DAH-noo
Tureinn	TEER-en

BIBLIOGRAPHY

Ashe, Geoffrey. *Mythology of the British Isles*. London: Methuen Press, 1990.

Backhouse, Janet. *Lindisfarne Gospels*. Oxford: Phaidon Press, 1986.

Bieler, Ludwig. *Ireland: Harbinger of the Middle Ages*. London: Oxford University Press, 1966.

Caldecott, Moyia. *Women in Celtic Myth*. Rochester, Vt.: Destiny Books, 1988.

Delaney, Frank. *The Celts*. Boston: Little, Brown and Company, 1986.

————. *Legends of the Celts*. New York: Sterling Press, 1991.

Gantz, Jeffrey. *Early Irish Myths and Sagas*. London: Penguin Books, 1981.

————. *The Mabinogion*. London: Penguin Books, 1976.

Goscinny, Rene, and Albert Uderzo. *Asterix the Gaul*. London: Hodder and Stoughton, 1969.

Green, Miranda. *Dictionary of Celtic Myth and Legend*. London: Thames and Hudson, 1992.

Herm, Gerhard. *The Celts*. New York: St. Martin's Press, 1975.

Kinsella, Thomas. *The Tain*. Oxford: Oxford University Press, 1970.

MacCana, Proinsias. *Celtic Mythology*. New York: Peter Bedrick Books, 1985.

Megaw, Vincent. "The Shape Changers: Art of the Iron Age Celts." *Archaeology* 31 (May/June 1978): 30–43.

Piggott, Stuart. *The Druids*. New York: Praeger Publishers, 1975.

Rutherford, Ward. *Celtic Mythology*. New York: Sterling Publishers, 1990.

Sellner, Edward C. *Wisdom of the Celtic Saints*. Notre Dame, Ind.: Ave Maria Press, 1993.

Severy, Merle. "The Celts." *National Geographic* 151 (May 1977): 582–633.

Simpson, Jacqueline. *European Mythology*. New York: Peter Bedrick Books, 1987.

Stewart, R.J. *Celtic Gods, Celtic Goddesses*. London: Blandford Press, 1990.